1

The Ultimate Book for Busy English Teachers

ESL SPEAKING ACTIVITIES

SPECIAL EDITION

MARC ROCHE

ESL SPEAKING ACTIVITIES: THE ULTIMATE BOOK FOR BUSY ENGLISH TEACHERS

INTERMEDIATE TO ADVANCED CONVERSATION BOOK FOR ADULTS:

TEACHING ENGLISH AS A SECOND LANGUAGE BOOK 1

ESL BOOKS FOR ADULTS: ADVANCED BOOK 1

MARC ROCHE

Sign up for exclusive ESL resources + free e-books + tons of other resources and goodies at the end of the book

Contents

11

GET MARC ROCHE'S STARTER LIBRARY FOR FREE

Sign up for the no-spam newsletter and get an introductory book and lots more exclusive content, all for free.

Details can be found at the end of the book.

ABOUT THIS ESL CONVERSATION BOOK FOR ADULTS

Make your TEFL lesson planning easier

"ESL Speaking Activities: The Ultimate Book for Busy English Teachers. Intermediate to Advanced Conversation Book for Adults" is jam-packed full of speaking cards, worksheets and conversation cards to whip out whenever you want and make your TEFL lesson plans instantly easier. It includes 100+ instant games & activities for Teaching English as a Second or Foreign Language Online & Offline.

Speaking is often the most intimidating part of English for many students, and it can be daunting as a teacher, when your students won't speak in class out of shyness or reluctance. This conversation book for adults will give you the tools needed to get students speaking, which will make your classes both more enjoyable and more productive!

In the Phrasal Verbs section of this book, you'll find grammar and vocabulary hand-outs before each set of speaking questions. You can do some of these handouts in class, or you can set them as homework if you prefer. They are ideal for preparing students for exams such as the Cambridge Business English exams, and other Cambridge exams like First Certificate and Advanced CAE, as well as IELTS and TOEFL.

ABOUT THE AUTHOR

Marc is originally from Manchester. He is a writer, teacher, trainer, and business manager. He has collaborated with organizations such as the British Council, the Royal Melbourne Institute of Technology and University of Technology Sydney among others. Marc has also worked with multinationals such as Nike, GlaxoSmithKline or Bolsas y Mercados.

Learn more about Marc at amazon.com/author/marcroche

OTHER BOOKS BY MARC ROCHE

Business Email: Write to Win. Business English & Professional Email Writing Essentials: How to Write Emails for Work, Including 100+ Business Email Templates

Business English Writing: Advanced Masterclass- How to Communicate Effectively & Communicate with Confidence

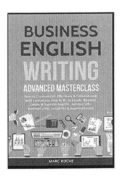

SECTION 1: ESL SPEAKING CARDS

These instant ESL conversation cards can be adapted into games, such as board games and other classroom activities to provide speaking practice and opportunities for feedback.

The teacher can use them with a timer if he or she wants to add some pressure to the activity, to make the activity more exciting and to prepare students for speaking, where time is a major factor. For example: students can work in pairs and speak for 1 to 2 minutes about each question as a mini-presentation type activity. Their partner can keep the time and provide feedback, while the teacher circulates the classroom and helps different pairs of students.

1. GOALS

What's your biggest goal at the moment and how do you plan to achieve it?	What is something you've never learned but wish you had?
What "short-term" goals do you have at the moment?	What "long term" goals do you have?
Think of a time when you didn't achieve one of your goals, describe the situation and how you felt.	Why are goals important? In your opinion, is it essential to have goals in life?
Have you got any goals that you think are unrealistic?	What is success to you? (What would be your definition of success?)

2. RESTAURANTS & FOOD

What's your favorite type of food? (Italian, Spanish, French, American, Mexican, Chinese, Thai etc..?)	Do you like to eat in restaurants? Describe the best restaurant you remember going to.
Are you a good cook? What's your star dish?	Describe the worst restaurant you remember going to.
Do you like 'junk food'?. Do you think 'junk food' should be more regulated by the government?	Have you ever eaten at an 'all you can eat' restaurant? Was the food as good as a normal restaurant?
What's the most important thing in a restaurant? 'Value for money', taste, atmosphere or décor?	What do you think about children crying in a restaurant when you are trying to eat? Does it bother you?

3. WORK

At what age would you like to retire? What do you think you will do after you retire?	What's the worst job you have ever done?
On a scale of 1- 10, how would rate your job? (10 the best and 1 the worst scores).	What changes would you introduce to improve your current job?
What's your dream job? (If money was not an issue, what job would you choose?)	If you won 'a gazillion' dollars in the lottery tomorrow, would you retire? How would you spend your time?
What jobs give people a high status in your country?	Would introducing a 4-day work-week be realistic in your country? Why or why not?

4. JOB INTERVIEWS

Is it important to be good at job interviews? Why or why not?	What skills, abilities and qualities do interviewers generally look for in a candidate?
On a scale of 1- 10, how would rate your job interview skills?	Are job interviews a fair assessment of someone's skills and suitability for a job?
What are the most common job interview questions? Pick one and answer it with your partner.	How do you feel when you have to do a job interview?
How could employers make job interviews fairer for candidates?	What 3 pieces of advice would you give someone who is about to do a job interview?

5. INVENTIONS

What are the most important inventions of the 20th and 21st centuries in your opinion?	How did the invention of the TV change people's lives?
How has the internet changed people's lives? Has it been a positive or a negative change?	What do you think is the worst invention in history?
Which two inventions would you like to see in the next 10 or 15 years? Why?	If someone invented a time machine, what time would you like to visit? Why?
How has the Internet influenced communication, correspondence and access to information?	What would you invent if you were a scientist? Why?

6. BODY LANGUAGE

Why do you think body language is important?	How do you use body language to communicate?
What type of body language is considered threatening in your culture?	What type of body language is considered threatening in your culture?
What type of body language is not allowed or *frowned upon* in your culture?	Do you try to use body language when you communicate in English?
In what situations can you misinterpret someone's body language?	Do you use the same amount of eye contact with men and women? Why or why not?

7. SPORTS

Do you play or watch any sports?	Do you think everybody should practice sports?
How often do you exercise?	Have you ever tried any extreme sports? Which ones? Which ones would you like to try?
What do you think is the most popular sport in the world?	What is your favorite team sport?
What is your favorite sport team?	Do professional athletes get paid too much? Why? Why not?

8. HOBBIES

What's your favorite hobby and how long have you been doing it?	What hobbies do you have?
Do you think it's important for people to have hobbies? Why or why not?	Is cost an important factor to consider when choosing a new hobby?
Which hobbies are the most popular in your country?	What's your opinion on hunting as a hobby?
Are there any hobbies you would like to try?	What's the most dangerous hobby you can think of?

9. MUSIC & MOVIES

What kind of music do you like?	What kinds of music don't you like?
Name one of your favorite songs of all time. What does this song remind you of?	Do you like to watch TV?
What are your favorite kinds of programs or shows right now?	Do you like movies?
What's your all-time favorite movie? When did you first watch it?	Who are your favorite actors or actresses?

10. CRIME

Are some parts of your home-town considered more dangerous than others? Which parts?	Do you ever get apprehensive about walking outside after dark?
Is gun control a good idea? Explain your opinion.	Should people who use illegal drugs be put in jail?
Would the legalization of drugs help lower crime rates?	Does prison help rehabilitate inmates? Should it?
What crimes do you think will increase in the future? Why?	What crimes do you think will decrease in the future?

11. CULTURE

What sort of things define a culture? E.g: language, beliefs, music etc..?	What advice would you give to a tourist visiting your country for the first time?
In your opinion, what is the most interesting thing about your culture? Why?	Is "when in Rome, do as the Romans do" good advice for someone traveling abroad? Explain.
What do you like about your culture?	Have you ever felt confused by the behavior of someone from another country? Explain.
What don't you like about your culture?	What is the most important thing your culture has contributed to the world?

12. MANNERS

Do bad mannered people bother you?	In your opinion, what's the best way to teach good manners to children?
What things are considered bad mannered in your culture? Why?	What things are considered good manners in your culture?
Is it important for children to have good manners, or should they express themselves freely?	Are people in your hometown or city polite on the road (when they drive)?
How can you be more polite when you drive?	Can manners affect your level of success in life? Explain your answer.

13. CREATIVITY

In your opinion, what is creativity?	Do you consider yourself creative? Explain your answer.
Do you think creativity can be learned or are people born with it?	Do you think more emphasis should be placed on creativity at school?
Discuss ideas for a device that would make people's lives easier.	Do you think you need to take risks in order to be creative?
In your opinion, who are some of the most creative musicians and writers in the last 20 years?	Can creativity help you in your career prospects? Explain.

14. DATING

Describe your ideal date with someone.	Describe your ideal person to go on a date with.
Do you "go Dutch" when dating, or do you think one of the people on the date should pay?	Have you ever been, or would you ever go on a 'blind date'?
Do you believe in 'love at first sight'? Explain.	What's the biggest 'crush' you've ever had on someone? Was it mutual?
Do perfect relationships exist?	What are some good conversation topics to talk about on a first date?

15. MEANING OF EDUCATION

Spontaneous Debates: The Meaning of Education

Optional Instructions for the teacher:

1. Hand out the debate cards face down (1 set for each group)

2. Assign a Discussion Leader

3. Optional: Assign students with "Agree" or "Disagree" roles at random. This often makes things more interesting as students find they have to play devil's advocate at times

4. Students pick up a card and turn it over.

5. They have 2 minutes to write an individual response. If their role is "Agree" they have to construct an argument agreeing with the statement. If their role is "Disagree", they construct an argument disagreeing with the statement

6. After prep time is up, they debate the topic for around 2 minutes. When you stop the debate you can ask students to discuss their "real opinions" for a minute before moving onto the next card.

Online Education will one day replace traditional schools and universities.	There is too much pressure on students and young employees in your country.
University education should be compulsory for everyone	People should get a job for a year before they go to university.
Voting for a politician who didn't go to university wouldn't be sensible.	Home schooling is better than public schooling.
A 'top class' education guarantees a good job.	Teachers should be paid more!

16. VALUE OF EDUCATION

Spontaneous Debates: The Value of Education

Optional Instructions for the teacher:

1. Hand out the debate cards face down (1 set for each group)

2. Assign a Discussion Leader

3. Optional: Assign students with "Agree" or "Disagree" roles at random. This often makes things more interesting as students find they have to play devil's advocate at times

4. Students pick up a card and turn it over.

5. They have 2 minutes to write an individual response. If their role is "Agree" they have to construct an argument agreeing with the statement. If their role is "Disagree", they construct an argument disagreeing with the statement

6. After prep time is up, they debate the topic for around 2 minutes. When you stop the debate you can ask students to discuss their "real opinions" for a minute before moving onto the next card.

The government should offer full funding to students who want to study.	Governments of developed nations should offer students from developing nations full funding.
If private universities break the law they should be forced to close.	Schools and universities shouldn't ban mobile phones in class.
Social skills are as important as good grades.	The internet has had a terrible effect on people's level of knowledge and social skills.
Universities should be more practical and offer 'a year in industry'.	Everybody should learn English.

17. POLITICS

Spontaneous Debates: Cross-cultural Communication

Optional Instructions for the teacher:

1. Hand out the debate cards face down (1 set for each group)

2. Assign a Discussion Leader

3. Optional: Assign students with "Agree" or "Disagree" roles at random. This often makes things more interesting as students find they have to play devil's advocate at times

4. Students pick up a card and turn it over.

5. They have 2 minutes to write an individual response. If their role is "Agree" they have to construct an argument agreeing with the statement. If their role is "Disagree", they construct an argument disagreeing with the statement

6. After prep time is up, they debate the topic for around 2 minutes. When you stop the debate you can ask students to discuss their "real opinions" for a minute before moving onto the next card.

16-year olds should be allowed to vote. They are mature and responsible enough.	Multi-cultural societies are dangerous as they can lead to cultural misunderstandings.
Cities like NY, Paris, Madrid, Barcelona & London have high crime because of immigration.	Extremist beliefs are sometimes necessary and good.
Political parties shouldn't be allowed to accept donations from private enterprises.	Voting is a waste of time.
Voting should be compulsory.	All politicians should have a university degree and special training to take part in politics.

18. HAVE YOU EVER.... ?

Have you ever cheated in an exam?	Have you ever forgotten someone's birthday?
Have you ever given a false excuse to get out of something? Describe the situation.	Have you ever tried any extreme sports? Which ones would you like to try in future?
Have you ever been to Thailand? Which countries would you most like to visit and why?	Have you ever been stuck in an elevator?
Have you ever received a present that you loved? What was it?	Have you ever received a present that you hated? What was it?

19. MEETING PEOPLE

Do you like meeting new people? Why?	What are some good questions to ask someone you just met?
Do you feel nervous when you meet new people?	What are some questions you shouldn't ask people you just met?
How can you quickly create rapport with new people you meet?	What kind of people do you like to meet?
Do people in your country use a lot of body language when they speak?	Describe the advantages of meeting people when you move to a new country.

20. LIVING ABROAD

Have you ever lived abroad? / How can living abroad change a person?	Which country or continents would you like to live in?
What would you miss most if you had to live abroad for some time?	Why do you think some people live abroad?
What do you believe would be the most difficult part of living in another country?	Do you think everyone should live in another country at least once in their life?
How is living abroad different from having a holiday abroad?	Do you know anyone who has decided to live abroad for good?

21. SPACE EXPLORATION

How does space research benefit the people?	Are we alone in the universe? Explain your opinion.
What progress do you estimate space research will achieve over the next two decades?	Would you consider traveling into space?
Is your country involved in space exploration?	Do you think that it is worth spending so much money on space exploration?
What aspects of our universe interest you most?	Should astronomy be taught in schools? What is your opinion?

22. FOOD

What is your country/region's traditional dish?	What kind of new food would you like to try?
Why does food play an important role in celebrations?	What are the advantages and disadvantages of Genetically Modified Food?
In what way is food important in our lives?	Would you buy Genetically Modified Food?
How popular is organic food in your country?	What would you say is your favorite kind of food?

23. COOKING

Do you think that traditional home cooking is a thing of the past?	How much do you like cooking?
What do you think is easier to make: food or desert?	How important is it for men to know how to cook?
Who taught you how to cook?	Do you have home cooked food every day of the week?
Why do you think the most famous chefs are men?	Should cooking be taught at school?

63

24. TRAVELLING

How has technology affected the way we travel?	What benefits are there to travelling?
How does travelling contribute to international understanding?	Should we travel our own country before travelling abroad?
Are there any risks to travelling to another country?	Do you prefer to travel in organized groups or independently?
What is the worst experience you have had when travelling?	What is your favorite means to travel very long distances?

25. SHOPPING

What's your favorite store for clothes, books, music, etc.? What do you like about it?	Do you shop in small shops, like boutiques, or do you go to the big department stores?
Do you tend to wait for the sales to look for bargains?	Have you found a good bargain recently? What was it?
Why do people go window-shopping?	What is the most unusual item you have ever bought?
Do you feel that global chain stores spoil the character of a town?	How often do you make impulse purchases?

26. FASHION

What are some of the latest fashion trends where you live?	Do you consider yourself fashionable?
How would you describe the working life of a fashion model?	Why do you think some clothing comes back into fashion again after 20 or 30 years?
Are the prices of some designer clothing justified?	Which city in your country would say is the most fashion conscious?
Who is the best dressed person in your family?	Which fashion accessories are most important to you?

27. WEATHER

How has the weather changed in your region over the last few years?	What is the coldest and hottest temperature you have ever experienced?
How can the weather affect a person's mood?	Do prefer to live in a hot or a cold climate?
What is your favorite kind of weather?	How does the weather affect our lifestyle?
Have you ever experienced extreme weather, such as hurricanes, flooding, etc.?	For how many days is the weather forecast in your country accurate? One, three, more?

28. ANIMALS

What animals, birds and insects can you see where you live – in your garden and in your area?	What would you do if you found an injured animal or bird by the side of the road?
What should we do about endangered species such as the blue whale, the cheetah, and the snow leopard?	Have you ever seen wild animals up close?
Is it cruel to lock up animals and birds behind bars in zoos and safari parks?	Which animal is the best pet to have?
Which animal do you identify with?	What is your country's national animal? Why was it chosen?

29. DRIVING

What kind of car do you drive?	Have you ever suffered from road rage?
Why do you think many people prefer driving to using public transport?	Will we all still be driving cars in 30 years' time?
How do you feel about driverless cars?	What is should be the legal age for someone to get a driving license?
What is the longest car trip you have been on?	How would you describe the driving behavior of people in your country?

30. THE HUMAN BODY

What makes a person attractive?	If you could swap bodies with somebody else for one day, who would it be?
Would you like your body to be cryogenically frozen when you die?	What are the pros and cons of tattoos and body piercings?
Would you ever consider having plastic surgery?	What do you like the most / the least about your body?
What do you do to look after your body?	Which part of your body is the most sensitive to illness or pain?

31. COLORS AND NUMBERS

What numbers or dates are important to you?	Do you prefer color or black and white films and photographs?
What number do you consider a lucky number?	What color clothes and shoes do you prefer? Why?
Do you have one favorite color, or different favorite colors for different things?	How can different colors affect our mood? How?
What do you think it would be like to be color blind?	Do you think different cultures have different meanings for colors?

32. FAMILY

How often do you see your grandparents or extended family?	Which member of your family are you closest to?
How important are families to society?	How is family life different now, compared to 100 years ago?
Would you like to know you family tree?	What would say is the ideal number of children for a family?
What roles should different members of a family have in a household?	How would you describe the perfect family?

33. HOME

Describe your dream home.	If there was a fire at your home, what would you rescue first?
What would you do if you lost your home and became homeless?	What is your favorite room in your home?
Many people say that their home is their sanctuary. Is this true for you?	What kind of relationship do you have with your neighbors?
Do you think it is better to rent or to own your home?	How important is it for you to keep your house perfectly clean and tidy?

34. Free Time

How would you describe your ideal weekend?	What is your favorite activity to do after a long day at work or school?
Do you have more, or less free time compared to your parents when they were your age?	Do you think you use your free time wisely?
What activity would you like to try that you haven't tried yet?	Do you prefer to spend you free time on your own, or with others?
What would be the ideal amount of free time per day?	What stage(s) in our life do you think we have the most/least free time?

35. PUBLIC TRANSPORT

What is the biggest problem with public transport in your town or city?	How do you think transport will be different in fifty years' time?
What is your favorite mode of public transport?	What is the most popular form of transport in your city/country?
Why do you think not everyone is using public transport?	Do you think that governments should encourage public transportation more?
How safe is it for people to use public transport in your city at all hours of the day and night?	How good is the public transportation in your city?

37. HOSPITAL

Have you or any member of your family ever been to hospital?	Do you believe that all healthcare should be free?
Which groups of people need to use hospitals the most often?	If a close friend or relative needed you to donate a kidney for a kidney transplant, would you do it?
In what ways can your local hospital be improved?	Would you ever consider going to hospital for non-essential treatment, like cosmetic surgery?
What do you think is the easiest job in a hospital?	What do you think is the worst job in a hospital?

38. PROBLEMS

What is a challenge you have faced and overcome recently?	Would you rather have ten small problems or one big problem?
What social problems are your country/region facing at the moment?	When did you last help somebody with their problems?
Do you think most people bring their problems upon themselves?	Would you ever write on an internet forum for advice?
Would you consider training to become a counsellor, and helping people for a living?	Do you have any heroes that have overcome problems in their lives and done something amazing?

39. MEDIA

If you could keep only one form of media, which would you choose?	Is there such a thing as an unbiased source of news?
Radio is over a hundred years old. Why hasn't it ever been replaced by a more modern form of media?	What would happen if the media just stopped?
How influenced are you by the media?	How can students use different parts of the media to improve their language skills?
Should the government control the press?	Are newspapers becoming obsolete?

40. HOTELS

Would you like to work in a hotel?	What are the advantages and disadvantages of staying in a hotel?
Do you use the spa and leisure facilities when you stay at a hotel?	If you were the manager of an old two-star hotel that was in danger of closure, how would you try to make it profitable again?
How would you describe a typical day's work of a hotel receptionist?	What is your opinion of large, all-inclusive resort hotels?
Do you think it is acceptable to take things such as bathrobes, soap, etc, from a hotel room when you leave?	Does your behavior differ when staying in a hotel compared to when you are at home?

41. LANGUAGES

What are the advantages and disadvantages of English becoming a global language?	Which language do you think would be the best global language?
What body language do you use in your culture?	Is preserving a dying language as important as preserving an endangered species?
Apart from English, which other language would you like to learn?	Do you agree that English is essential for success in one's career?
What age is the best to start learning a new language?	What is more important when speaking a foreign language: fluency or accuracy?

42. TECHNOLOGY

Has technology made our lives more complicated?	Do technological advances increase the gap between rich and poor?
Which areas of technology are the most important to teach at school?	Which invention has had a more positive impact on our lives: the mobile phone or personal computer?
Do you agree that technology has made us lazy?	Do you believe that advances in technology causes job losses?
If mobile phones disappeared one day, how do you think people would cope?	In your opinion, which industry has been most transformed by technology?

43. ART

How would you describe your relationship with art?	What paintings, drawings, or sculptures do you have in your home?
Is collecting works of art a good investment?	What's the point in owning a valuable piece of art if it has to be kept locked away?
Do you go to art exhibitions, galleries, antique markets?	What is your definition of art?
Who is the most famous artist from your country?	Is there any public art in your city?

44. HISTORY

Do you think it is important to have a knowledge of history?	What period of history would you like to learn more about?
Should history lessons focus on politics and war, or on social changes?	Which local historical figure has had the greatest impact on your country?
What do you think of the recent history of your country, the past 30 years?	Which historical figure would you like to meet?
Do you think history repeats itself?	Are you proud of the history of your country?

45. BOOKS

How important is reading books?	What should be the roles of libraries in modern life?
If you could write a book, what kind of book (genre) would it be?	Would you go to bookshops more often if they were friendly places with comfortable armchairs and coffee shops?
Could you live in a world without books?	What is the worst book that you've ever read?
Have you read more than one book by the same author?	How can we encourage children to read more?

SECTION 2: BUSINESS ENGLISH CONVERSATION QUESTIONS

These instant conversation worksheets can be adapted into games, such as board games and other classroom activities to provide speaking practice and opportunities for feedback.

The teacher can also use them with a timer if he or she wants to add some pressure to the activity, to make the activity more exciting or to prepare students for an exam such as Cambridge Business, where time is a factor. For example: students can work in pairs and speak for 1 to 2 minutes about each question as a mini-presentation type activity. Their partner can keep the time and provide feedback, while the teacher circulates the classroom and helps different pairs of students.

1.WORK

What do you do?

What does your job position entail?

Can you describe your tasks on a daily basis?

What is your favorite task at work?

What is your least favorite task at work?

How would you describe your current job?

2. DAYS OFF

How many days do you work in a week?

How many hours do you work in a day?

How many days do you work in a year?

How many vacation leaves do you have?

How many sick leaves do you have?

How many days off do you have in a week?

How many days off do you have in a month?

What do you do during your day off?

What do you do during your vacation leave?

3. AGE AT WORK

At what age did you start working?

What is the ideal age for someone to start working?

What is the ideal age for someone to stop working?

At what age would you want to retire?

At what age do people start working in your country?

At what age do people retire in your country?

4. JOB LOCATION

What jobs are available in your hometown?

What will make you consider working in your hometown?

Why did you choose to work in your hometown?

What jobs are available in your city?

What will make you consider working in the city?

Why did you choose to work in the city?

What is the most popular city in your country in terms of job hunting?

What is the most sought-after business center in your country?

What is the ideal city for you to work in?

5. WORKING FROM HOME

In your own words, how would you define working from home?

What is a good excuse to work from home?

How do you stay productive working from home?

What are the benefits of working from home?

What are the disadvantages of working from home?

What would it take for you to permanently work from home?

How popular are work from home jobs in your country?

Should working from home be an option for all office workers?

6. OFFICE LOCATION

How far do you live from your office?

How many hours do you commute in total per week?

What mode of transportation do you use to get to work?

How much time do you spend in traffic?

How much do you spend on transportation?

Would you consider renting an apartment near your office?

How far is your office from the nearest mall?

How far is your office from the nearest park?

How far is your office from the nearest hang out place?

How far is your office from the nearest train station?

How far is your office from the nearest bus stop?

How many floors does your work building have?

7. WORKING OVERSEAS

How would you consider working overseas?

In your opinion/experience, what is the best country to work in?

In your opinion/experience, what is the worst country to work in?

If you were given a chance, which country would you like to work in?

What would you consider before working overseas?

Why do some people prefer to work abroad?

What type of people are ideal for working overseas?

What type of people do you think would not be successful working overseas?

8. OFFICE LUNCH

Where do you usually eat out during lunch break?

How often do you usually take for your lunch break?

Who do you eat out with at work?

When do you usually eat out at work?

How much do you usually spend when you eat out at work?

What do you usually order when you eat out at work?

Why do people prefer eating out than eating in the office?

Why do some people prefer eating home cooked meals in the office than eating out?

9. AFTER WORK ACTIVITIES

Where do you usually hang out after work?

How often do you usually hang out after work?

Who do you hang out with after work?

How much do you usually spend when you hang out with your co-workers?

How far is the nearest place where you can hang out?

Why do so many people hangout after work?

Why do many people choose not to hangout after work?

In your country, what is the most common hangout activity after work?

10. REWARDS AND RECOGNITION

Why should employers recognize employees' efforts?

How are employees recognized for their achievements in your office?

How should an employer recognize an employee?

When was the last time an employee was recognized in your office?

When was the last time you were recognized at work?

How would you feel if you were recognized for the quality of your work? What reward would you like to receive?

11. TEAM BUILDING

Why is it important to have team building activities? Who benefits the most in team building, employees or employers?

When was the last time you participated in a team building activity?

What is the best team building activity in your opinion?

What is your least favorite team building activity?

How does team building help a business/company?

Who should choose the venue of the team building exercises? Why?

Who should choose the activities of the team building exercises? Why?

12. OFFICE SUPPLIES AND EQUIPMENT

What office supplies do you have at your desk?

What office supplies do you often use?

What office supplies do you seldom use?

What office supplies would you like to be available in your company?

13. WORKING HOURS

What do you think about 9 to 5 jobs? Would you prefer a different time-table? Why?

In your opinion, how many hours should someone work in a day? Why?

In your opinion, how many days should someone work in a week? Why?

14. OVERTIME

When was the last time you worked overtime?

How many hours do you usually work overtime?

How many hours was your longest overtime?

Should companies be able to force employees to work overtime?

Should companies be forced to pay employees for any overtime they work?

15. BUSINESS TRIPS

What are the advantages and disadvantages of frequent business travel?

Would you like to travel as part of your job?

How often do you go on business trips?

When and where was your last business trip?

What is your most memorable business trip?

Which country would you most like to visit in your next business trip?

Which country would you least like to visit again in your next business trip?

How do you feel about business trips?

Why are business trips important?

16. EXPERIENCE

How long have you been in your current company?

How long do you plan to stay with your current company?

How long did you stay with your first company?

In your country, how common is it to stay with a company for a long time?

What professional experience has been the most important in your career so far? Why?

17. PROMOTION & DEMOTION

When was your last promotion?

When are you expecting to get a promotion?

How old is your oldest co-worker?

How young is your youngest co-worker?

How important is getting a promotion to you?

What is the best way to be promoted?

How can office politics affect promotion?

What would be your reaction if you got promoted tomorrow?

How common is demotion in your company?

Why would someone get demoted?

18.PROBATIONARY PERIOD:

How long is your company's probationary period?

How long did it take for you to get a permanent position?

What are the differences between a regular employee and someone on probation?

Are there any ways for someone to be made permanent faster? What are they?

19. CONTRACTS

How many workers do you have in your company?

How common are permanent contracts in your country?

How do you feel about the general way companies contract workers in your country?

Who benefits more from contracts, the worker or the company?

Would you consider working under a third-party agency?

Why do people consider working under third party agencies?

Why do companies hire from third party agencies?

What are the benefits of hiring workers from third party agencies?

If you were a business owner, would you consider hiring workers from third party agencies? Why?

How long should an employee be under probation?

20. WORK-LIFE BALANCE

In your own words, how would you define work-life balance?

How important is work-life balance? Why?

Who benefits from work-life balance?

How can you achieve work-life balance in your life?

How much work-life balance do you currently have?

What initiatives does your company have with regards to work-life balance?

How can the government help in achieving work-life balance for workers in your country or region?

Describe someone you know who has a great work-life balance.

For you, what activities help in achieving work-life balance?

21. MANAGEMENT & LEADERSHIP

What are the advantages of being a boss?

What are the disadvantages of being a boss?

What are some qualities of a good boss?

What are some qualities of a bad boss?

Who is the best boss you've ever had?

How often do you talk to your boss?

How often does your boss check on you?

How often does your boss hangout with your team?

What are the traits you like most about your current boss?

How common is it in your country for employees to address their bosses with sir/ma'am?

If you were given a choice, would you like to be given more management responsibilies? Why?

What does your boss say when you come in late for work?

In your own words, how would you define a leader?

Is there a difference between a manager and a leader? Why?

Is it necessary to be a good leader in order to be a good manager?

22. BEING AN EMPLOYEE

What was your very first job?

When did you land your first job?

What are the advantages of being a normal employee and not having any people management duties?

What are the disadvantages of being a normal employee and not having any people management duties?

Would you like to have one job for your whole life with a good, steady salary or do you need change to stay motivated?

23. FREELANCING

How common is freelancing in your country?

Why do some people choose to work as freelancers?

What are the advantages of working as a freelancer?

What are the disadvantages of working as a freelancer?

What is the best thing about being a freelancer?

What is the worst thing about working as a freelancer?

If you were given a chance, would you work as a freelancer? Why?

What are the most common jobs of freelancers?

24. DIFFERENT PROFESSIONS

What are some examples of professions that suit your personality?

What is the worst job you can think of for your personality?

What are the most prestigious professions in your country? Why?

Who do you think should be the most well paid in terms of jobs?

Who do you think should be the least paid in terms of jobs?

What was your dream job when you were a kid?

What is your dream job now?

Given the opportunity, would you pursue your dream job? Why or why not?

How well paid are politicians in your country?

What is the most in demand job in your
country?

25. JOB REQUIREMENTS

How important is educational achievement when applying for a job in your country?

Which is more important, qualifications or experience? Why?

How important is experience when applying for a job in your country?

In your country, how challenging is it to find a job for newly graduated candidates?

Was it difficult to get your first job?

What assistance do recent graduates get from the government when applying for jobs?

26. JOB INTERVIEWS

How was your first ever interview? Describe your experience. What did you do well and what did you do badly?

How do you feel during interviews?

How do you prepare before your interviews?

What clothes do you wear in interviews?

How important are first impressions in interviews?

What makes you stand out from other applicants when you apply for a job? (What are your strong points?)

What's your biggest weakness?

How do you see your career evolving in the next 2 years?

Do you think job interviews are a fair assessment of a candidate's suitability for a job?

If you were an interviewer, what you look for in an applicant?

27. BENEFITS & PERKS

What do you look for in a company?

Rank the following benefits and perks in order of importance for you. Explain your answers:

- Frequent travel
- Management responsibilities
- Child-care benefits
- Long holidays
- Travel and food allowances
- Frequent social events and activities organized by the company
- The option to work from home

What benefits and perks would you most like to have in your current position?

28. RESIGNATION

What is the most common reason for someone to resign?

What was the reason why you left your previous job?

What's the difference between termination and resignation?

Would you ever consider leaving your current position? What would it take for you to leave?

How would you feel if your closest co-worker resigned?

How would you feel if your current boss resigned?

How do you think your co-workers would feel if you resigned?

How do you think your boss would feel if you resigned?

29. JOB-HOPPING

How many jobs have you had in the past five years?

How common is it for people to change jobs in your country?

What do you think about job-hopping?

Why do some people job-hop?

How can job-hopping affect your career?

30. SALARY

How do you feel about your first ever salary?

What is your ideal salary? Why?

How important is salary in applying for a job?

What is the common salary range for your chosen profession?

How important are salary increases for staff motivation?

Is salary the most important factor in a job?

Would you rather do something you love for a low salary or something you hate for a high salary? Why?

Is it good for governments to introduce laws to guarantee a minimum wage? Why or why not?

31. CHOOSING A COMPANY

What is the most effective way of finding jobs? Why?

What are the factors you consider when choosing a company?

How important is company image in choosing a company?

How important is location when choosing a company?

How important is personal growth when choosing a company?

How important is professional growth when choosing a company?

How important is diversity when choosing a company?

32. FEELINGS ABOUT YOUR JOB

How much do you like your job? (Be as sincere as possible!)

Why do you (or don't you) like your job?

What is your favorite part about your job?

33. CO-WORKERS

What kind of people do you like to work with?

What kind of people are you working with now?

Who do you prefer working with, young or old employees?

Who do you prefer working with, male or female employees?

Would you consider yourself a workaholic? Why?

Would you consider yourself easy going? Why?

What do you think about people who are easy going in their jobs?

34. RETIREMENT

When do you plan to retire?

Why do you think some people never want to retire and others can't wait to retire?

What is your ideal retirement?

At what age do people in your country usually retire?

Where would you like to spend your retirement?

35. EMAIL

How many emails do you receive in a day?

How helpful is emailing in your job?

Why is it sometimes easier to have misunderstandings with people during email exchanges?

Do you sometimes feel overwhelmed by the number of emails in your inbox? Do you have any tricks to tackle this problem?

What are the advantages and disadvantages of using office memos to communicate with staff?

36. MEETINGS

How do you feel about meetings?

When was the last time you attended a meeting?

What do you think about lunch meetings?

Which do you prefer, formal or informal meetings? Why?

Have you ever 'dozed off' while in a meeting?

When was the last time you dozed off in a meeting?

Do you prefer traditional meetings or teleconferences?

37. CONFERENCES

How many conferences do you have in a year?

How do you feel about conferences?

Describe the last conference you attended.

38. TECHNOLOGY

How often do you answer phone calls in your current job?

How often do you use your cellphone at work?

What kind of technology do you use at the office?

How has technology changed the way we work?

How has technology changed the way we learn?

39. OFFICE ENVIRONMENT

How would you describe your current office environment?

How important is office environment?

What is your ideal work environment?

How many co-workers can you count as friends?

How do you feel about office politics?

How rampant is office politics in your company?

SECTION 3: PHRASAL VERBS (VOCABULARY, GRAMMAR & SPEAKING)

In this section, you'll find grammar and vocabulary hand-outs and worksheets before each set of speaking questions. You can do some of these handouts in class with students, or you can set them as homework if you prefer. They are ideal for preparing students for exams such as the First Certificate, Advanced CAE, IELTS and TOEFL.

All the worksheets and ESL conversation cards can be photocopied and used in the classroom and have been designed to be adapted to classroom games and warmers.

STUDENT HANDOUT: INTRODUCTION TO PHRASAL VERBS

What is a phrasal verb?

A phrasal verb is a group of two or more words, which performs the same function as other verbs. It is formed by a main verb and an adverb, a preposition or both.

It's like a deliciously confusing word sandwich.

[Main Verb] + adverb/preposition/adverb and preposition = phrasal verb

Phrasal verbs are unique to English and other Germanic languages and can cause issues for English learners. They can be transitive (they take a direct object), intransitive (they do not take a direct object), separable (they can be separated) and inseparable (they cannot be separated). We will cover the differences between these, complete with descriptions and exercises, later on.

Although the meanings differ, phrasal verbs are conjugated just like main verbs. For example:

The car breaks down.

The car broke down.

Here are some common phrasal verbs to get you started:

154

Phrasal Verb bring up

Example He brought up the fact that I was too short to go on the rollercoaster.

Meaning: to mention a topic

Phrasal Verb call off

Example She called off the wedding.

Meaning: to cancel

Phrasal Verb carry on

Example The bag was heavy, and my feet hurt, but I carried on with the walk.

Meaning: to continue

Phrasal Verb deal with

Example I can't deal with stress.

Meaning: to handle

Phrasal Verb end up

Example They ended up in Sheffield.

155

Meaning: to reach a state or place

Phrasal Verb   fall through

Example *Our plans to meet for coffee fell through.*

Meaning: to not happen

Phrasal Verb get on with (something)

Example *She was busy, so I got on with my essay.*

Meaning: to continue to do

Phrasal Verb hand in

Example *I handed in my thesis.*

Meaning: to submit

Phrasal Verb join in

Example *She joined in the conversation at the party.*

Meaning: to participate

Phrasal Verb keep up with

Example *My boss talks too fast and I can't keep up.*

Meaning: to stay at the same pace or level.

Phrasal Verb let down

Example *She was supposed to collect me at 6:00 but she didn't. She really let me down.*

Meaning: to disappoint

Phrasal Verb look forward to

Example *Are you looking forward to your holiday?*

Meaning: to be excited about something, to anticipate something good.

Phrasal Verb mix up

Example *I can't tell the twins apart; I always mix up their names.*

Meaning: to mistake one thing for another

Phrasal Verb pass away

Example *My grandfather passed away last night.*

Meaning: to die

Phrasal Verb put off

Example *I kept putting it off, even though I knew I had to do it*

Meaning: to postpone

Phrasal Verb rule out

Example We know it wasn't John who ate Sarah's pasta, so we can rule him out

Meaning: to eliminate

Phrasal Verb stick up for (someone)

Example *Catherine was always getting bullied, so Alex stuck up for her.*

Meaning: to defend

Important Note: Don't get confused with the adjective "stuck up" in English. "Stuck up" has no connection to the phrasal verb "stick up for". As an adjective, "stuck up" means arrogant, distant or feeling superior. For example: *Mary is quite stuck up, she kept criticizing our neighborhood all the time even though she used to live here!*

Phrasal Verb think over

Example Janine told Roger that she would have to think over his proposal.

Meaning: to consider

Phrasal Verb work out

Example

1. It's important for your fitness that you work out three times a week.

2. The Math problem was difficult, but I eventually worked it out.

Meaning:

1. to do physical exercise

2. to solve a problem

STUDENT HANDOUT

How can I learn vocabulary and phrasal verbs?

The first thing you need to understand is you should never try to memorize long lists, out of context. To learn a word well, you need to see it, understand it, learn how it works in sentences and then use it.

Focus on one phrasal verb per day. Learn it in the morning, then throughout the day think of various sentences where you could use that verb. If you do this, you could DOMINATE 365 phrasal verbs by the end of this year. Think about it.

The more English media you consume, the more phrasal verbs you will learn, but as with any item of vocabulary, you will have to learn them individually.

Study, study, study. Search for new phrasal verbs, and study them every day until you know them. Make notes of the phrasal verbs using sentences in a clean notebook. Never just write it down, it's a waste of time. Write the phrasal verb down and them write a sentence using that phrasal verb. Then, the next day, write ANOTHER sentence using the same phrasal verb and so on.

Use them. Try to participate in real English conversations as often as possible so that you can get experience and gain confidence using phrasal verbs. If you are shy, don't let that "get you down", remember that socializing in your own language is often hard when you meet new people, so speaking another language is even harder. Be patient with yourself and don't give up. If you need help, contact me.

As with any item of vocabulary, you will have to learn them individually. The more English media that you consume, the more phrasal verbs you will learn.

TASK 1

Try to match the phrasal verbs below with their synonyms:

Phrasal Verb *Example*

a. throw away *John threw away his apple core.*

b. look into *Sarah looked into the murder case.*

c. get away with *The robber got away with the crime.*

d. use up *Use up the washing-up liquid before you buy another bottle!*

e. run out of *My phone ran out of battery.*

Meanings:

1. use completely

2. exhaust supply

3. investigate

4. discard

5. escape blame

Check your answers.

ANSWERS

Task 1:

a)   4

b)   3

c)   5

d)   1

e)   2

When can I use Phrasal Verbs?

Phrasal verbs are used in non-formal situations. You will hear them used in speech on a daily basis, in emails between friends, and in some magazines. They are becoming more and more prevalent, but there are certain situations where you should avoid using them:

- Formal letters or emails.

- Academic papers or presentations.

TASK 2:

In the following email, underline all the phrasal verbs that you can find and write their meanings below. You may need to use a dictionary.

Hi Maria,

I'm sorry that I was late to work today. My car broke down yesterday, so I took the bus instead. However, the bus was held up in traffic! It seems that everyone was going to work at the same time!

Don't worry about the project, I'll be able to catch up with the rest of my colleagues. I'll drop by the office on the weekend and see if there is anything extra that I can do.

I hope you've got over your cold, I hear it's been going round the office recently.

Best wishes,

Ben

(1)   /

(2)   /

(3)   /

(4)   /

(5)   /

(6)   /

ANSWERS:

Task 2:

(1)   break down / to stop working

(2)   hold up / to delay (to be held up- to be delayed)

(3)   catch up / to do tasks

(4)   drop by / visit briefly

(5)   get over / to recover from an illness

(6)   go round / to affect a lot of people

Types of Phrasal Verb (Student Handout)

There are 4 types of phrasal verb:

Transitive phrasal verbs

Intransitive phrasal verbs

Separable phrasal verbs

Inseparable phrasal verbs

Transitive and Intransitive Phrasal Verbs

There are two types of verbs in English: Transitive and Intransitive. Transitive verbs take a direct object, whereas intransitive verbs do not.

Transitive phrasal verbs

These phrasal verbs take a direct object:

I look after my sister on Mondays

I	*look after*	+	*my sister*	*on Mondays*
	[phrasal verb]	+	[direct object]	

166

Intransitive phrasal verbs

These phrasal verbs do not take a direct object:

When I grow up, I want to be a firefighter.

When	*I*	*grow up*	*I want to be a firefighter*
		[phrasal verb]	

Task 1

Look at the phrasal verbs below in the table with their examples. Decide whether they are transitive or intransitive. (You can find the answers at the end of this section).

Phrasal Verb: Example

1. **Take out**   *Please take out the bins before you leave.*

2. **Cheer up**   *I need to cheer up my sister because she's crying.*

3. **Come back**   *I'm waiting for my mother to come back from the shops.*

4. **Go through**   *I went through my father's bottle of cologne.*

5. **Get up**   *I get up every morning at 6am.*

6. **Get by**   *It was a difficult year and Mrs Calloway lost her job, but they got by.*

167

7. **Pass out**   *She passed out because of the amount of pain she was suffering from.*

8. **Get along with**   *He gets along with most people.*

Task 2

Read the following sentences. They are all transitive. Underline the transitive verbs and highlight the direct object.

1. He is so creative; he made up a story for his daughter and her friends.

2. I have to fill out this form, so I can go to university.

3. Can you help me hang up this picture?

4. There was a problem with his essay; he had left out a conclusion.

5. The old friends ran into each other on the street.

6. I don't like how she looks down on everyone.

7. We tried on the costumes, but we looked awful in them!

8. She takes after her grandmother.

9. My mother says I have to get rid of my old toys.

10. I can't hear anything - please turn up the volume!

You can find the answers at the end of this section.

Separable and Inseparable Phrasal Verbs

As phrasal verbs consist of a main verb, an adverb or preposition or both, these verbs can sometimes be separated. Only transitive verbs (which take a direct object) can be separated.

Separable phrasal verbs

These phrasal verbs, as the name suggests, can be separated:

Turn off the light before you leave.

Turn the light off before you leave.

Only transitive phrasal verbs (which take a direct object) can be separated. However, it is important to remember:

All separable phrasal verbs are transitive, but not all transitive phrasal verbs are separable.

Turn off	+	*the light*	*before you leave.*
[Phrasal verb]	+	[direct object]	

169

Turn + *the light* + *off before you leave.*

[PV part 1] + [direct object] + [PV part 2]

Inseparable phrasal verbs

These phrasal verbs, as the name suggests, can't be separated:

He passed away last night.

He   *passed away*   *last night*

[inseparable verbs]

They cannot be separated due to the fact that there is no direct object. The phrase *'last night'* is an adverb.

Word Order

When separating phrasal verbs, there is a word order that must be adhered to:

- When referring to a specific object or person, the object can go between the phrasal verb or after the phrasal verb:

I picked up Sophie from school.

I picked Sophie up from school.

- When using a pronoun as the direct object, the pronoun can only go between the phrasal verb:

I picked her up from school.

Task 3

The following phrases are separable phrasal verbs. **Write out the different ways to separate the phrasal verb using correct word order.**

Example:

I hung up the picture on the wall.

I hung the picture up on the wall.

I hung it up on the wall.

1. She put out the fire.

....

....

....

....

2.   I called off the party.

....

....

....

....

3.   Oscar asked out Samantha.

....

....

....

....

4.   They handed in their essays on time.

....

....

....

....

5.   I like showing off my new boots.

....

....

....

....

6.   Turn off the washing machine!

....

....

....

....

7.   I have to drop off my sister at a party.

....

....

....

....

8.   She won't give up her love of singing.

....

....

....

....

9.   Put on your hat.

....

....

....

....

10.   I made up a lie.

....

....

....

....

Answers:

Task 1

1.   *Transitive*

2.   *Transitive*

3.   *Intransitive*

4.   *Transitive*

5.   *Intransitive*

6.   *Intransitive*

7.   *Intransitive*

8.   *Transitive*

Task 2

1.   *He is so creative; he made up a story for his daughter and her friends.*

2.   *I have to fill out this form, so I can go to university.*

176

3.   Can you help me hang up this picture?

4.   There was a problem with his essay; he had left out a conclusion.

5.   The old friends ran into each other on the street.

6.   I don't like how she looks down on everyone.

7.   We tried on the costumes, but we looked awful in them!

8.   She takes after her grandmother.

9.   My mother says I have to get rid of my old toys.

10.   I can't hear anything - please turn up the volume!

Task 3

1.   She put out the fire.

She put the fire out.

She put it out.

2.   I called off the party.

I called the party off.

I called it off.

3.   *Oscar asked out Samantha.*

Oscar asked Samantha out.

Oscar asked her out.

4.   *They handed in their essays on time.*

They handed their essays in on time.

They handed them in on time.

5.   *I like showing off my new boots.*

I like showing my new boots off.

I like showing them off.

6.   *Turn off the washing machine!*

Turn the washing machine off!

Turn it off!

7.   *I have to drop off my sister at a party.*

I have to drop my sister off at a party.

I have to drop her off at a party.

178

8.   *She won't give up her love of singing.*

She won't give her love of singing up.

She won't give it up.

9.   *Put on your hat.*

Put your hat on.

Put it on.

10.   *I made up a lie.*

I made a lie up.

I made it up.

TYPES OF PHRASAL VERBS (STUDENT HANDOUT 2)

Phrasal verbs can be frustrating to learn. They often bear little resemblance to the main verb and there are so many to learn with different meanings.

The best way to learn these is to learn 'clusters' of phrasal verbs.

For example, the verb 'take':

Phrasal Verb	Transitive/Intransitive? Separable/Inseparable?	Example	Meaning
take after	transitive, inseparable	With my brown eyes and black hair, I take after my mother.	Resemble
take back	intransitive, separable	You need to take this dress back to the shop.	Return
take care of	transitive, inseparable	1. She can't go on holiday; she has to take care of her little sister. 2. He can't afford a holiday; he has to take care of these bills first.	1. Provide care for 2. Accept responsibility for
take off	1. transitive, separable 2. transitive, separable 3. intransitive, inseparable	1. Take your hat off. 2. Holly took the day off because she was ill. 3. The rocket took off.	1. Remove 2. Arrange an absence from work 3. To leave or to depart (quickly)
take up	1. transitive, separable 2. transitive, separable	1. I've decided to take up knitting. 2. James took up two seats.	1. Begin a hobby 2. Occupy space

If you look in a large dictionary, you will be able to see the various phrasal verbs under the main verb. It is a good idea to learn these in groups.

Task 1

Match the phrasal verbs (1-6) with their meanings (a-f).

Phrasal Verbs with "Put"

Meanings:

180

a. Tolerate

b. Return to its rightful place

c. Allow someone to stay for the night

d. Save something for later

e. Postpone, delay

f. Wear something

'

1. Put away - Transitive, separable. Example: *I put away a little money each month for my savings.*

Meaning:

....

....

2. Put off - Transitive, separable. **Example:** I keep putting off my homework because there are more fun things to do!

Meaning:

....

....

3. Put on - Transitive, separable. **Example:** It's cold outside so I suggest you put on your jacket.

Meaning:

....

....

4. Put up- Transitive, separable. **Example:** My aunt and uncle are coming to London so I'm putting them up for the night.

Meaning:

....

....

5. Put up with- Transitive, inseparable. **Example:** I cannot put up with this nonsense any longer!

Meaning:

....

....

6. Put back- Transitive, inseparable. **Example:** I'm not buying you that toy so put it back.

Meaning:

....

....

You can find the answers at the end of this section.

Task 2

MORE PHRASAL VERBS WITH "PUT":

*a. I´m prepared to **put up with** it for the time being.*

*b. The World Wildlife Fund **put out** a press release.*

*c. Don´t **put off** until tomorrow what can be done today.*

*d. After my dog was **put down**, I cried for days.*

*e. He began to **put away** all the toys he had taken out to play with.*

*f. The Trade Union council **put forward** a plan for national recovery.*

*g. My self-confidence has been undermined because my mother is always **putting me down**.*

*h. I´ve got nowhere to sleep! Could anybody **put me up**?*

Match the phrasal verbs with their meanings. Put <u>one or two words</u> in each gap:

1. If you put something _____, you postpone it until a later time.

2. If you put something _____, you replace it somewhere tidily.

3. If you put an animal _____, you kill it because it is too old, or it is in too much pain.

183

4. If you put someone _____, you give them a bed for a night or two.

5. If you put _____ someone or something, you tolerate or accept them, even though that person or thing is disagreeable.

6. If you put someone _____, you criticize or humiliate them.

7. If you put _____ an idea or a proposal, you state or publish it, so people can consider and discuss it.

8. If a statement is put _____ to people, it is officially told to them.

Put a phrasal verb in each gap (!!!! Watch the tense)

1. I left my girlfriend because she´s always _____.

2. I _____ her moods if I were you.

3. If they _____ for the night, I would have had to sleep in the street.

4. Clinton has _____ a press release which contradicts his previous statements.

5. You needn´t _____ the meeting: everybody could have made it in the end.

6. Every day, the government _____ a new plan to tackle unemployment.

7. If they find stray dogs in the streets, the poor animals
_____.

8. As a child, I could never get used to _____ my things
_____ after I had used them.

Task 3

In this conversation between two friends (Jim and Sasha), underline the phrasal verbs and write their meanings below. You may need to use a dictionary.

Jim: I meant to call in on my granddad today, but he passed away last night.

Sasha: Oh, I'm sorry Jim. Were you looking after him?

Jim: No, my grandma was. I think she liked taking care of him.

Sasha: Are you going to go over later, to see how she is?

Jim: Yes, I'll visit her later. She's with my parents at the moment. I'll have to find out what the plan is.

Sasha: Why don't you come over to my place? We can order pizza, or if you'd prefer, we can eat out.

Jim: Sure, that's a good idea. I'm looking forward to it.

1..
....

2..
....

3..
....

4..
....

5..
....

6..
....

7..
....

8...
....

9...
....

You can find the answers at the end of this section.

THREE-WORD PHRASAL VERBS

We have already discussed four types of phrasal verbs: **transitive, intransitive, separable and inseparable**. Most of the phrasal verbs which we have studied in these sections have been two part: they are made up of a main verb and a preposition or an adverb. However, there are phrasal verbs with two particles. These are called **three-word phrasal verbs.**

Three-word Phrasal Verbs

These are **always transitive** due to the fact that they require a direct object and they are **only inseparable.**

We have already seen a few three-word phrasal verbs, but below are some additional ones for you to learn:

Phrasal Verb	Example	Meaning
Come up with	She came up with a great idea.	Contribute or think an idea, suggestion or plan
Get along with	He gets along with his dad.	Have a good relationship with
Talk back to	You must not talk back to your parents.	Answer impolitely to someone
Get away from	I need to book a holiday and get away with it all.	Take a break
Walk out on	I walked out on my family last year.	Abandon

Task 4:

The paragraph below does not use phrasal verbs. Using the three-word phrasal verbs from the table above, rewrite the story.

Three-word phrasal verbs from the table: *Come up with,*

get along with, talk back to, get away from, walk out on

I have never had a good relationship with my sister. She always answers impolitely to our parents. Last summer I grew sick of it. I needed to take a break from her, or I would go crazy! I thought of a plan that would help. I decided to abandon my family once and for all...

You can find the answers at the end of this section.

....

....

....

....

....

....

....

189

....

....

Task 5

Phrasal Verb	Meaning
Think back on	Recall
Look up to	Respect or admire
Cut down on	Curtail
Look out for	Be careful of
Make sure of	Verify

Using the three-word phrasal verbs in the table above (listed with their definitions), write the missing phrasal verbs in the sentences below.

Three-word phrasal verbs:

Think back on

Look up to

Cut down on

Look out for

Make sure of

190

1.   I am putting on weight, I need to
_____ my chocolate eating!

2.   She _____ her older brother.

3.   - Do you want to go on a walk in the countryside today?

     - Sure, but we'll have to _____ rattlesnakes!

4.   _____ the situation before you act.

5.   When I _____ our marriage, I remember all the good parts.

You can find the answers at the end of this section.

Answers:

Task 1

1. d

2. e

3. f

4. c

5. a

6. b

Task 2

1. If you put something off, you postpone it until a later time.

2. If you put something away, you place it somewhere tidily.

3. If you put an animal down, you kill it because it is too old, or it is in too much pain.

4. If you put someone up, you give them a bed for a night or two.

5. If you put up with someone or something, you tolerate or accept them, even though that person or thing is annoying or unpleasant.

6. If you put someone down, you criticize or humiliate them.

7. If you put forward an idea or a proposal, you state or publish it, so people can consider and discuss it.

8. If a statement is put out to people, it is officially told to them.

Put a phrasal verb in each gap (Watch the tense)

1. I left my girlfriend because she´s always putting me down.

2. I wouldn`t put up with her moods if I were you.

3. If they hadn`t put me up for the night, I would have had to sleep in the street.

4. Clinton has put out a press release which contradicts his previous statements.

5. You needn´t have put off the meeting: everybody could have made it in the end.

6. Every day, the government puts forward a new plan to tackle unemployment.

7. If they find stray dogs in the streets, the poor animals are put down.

8. As a child, I could never get used to putting my things away after I had used them.

Task 3

1. call in on - visit

2. passed away - died

3. looking after - care for

4. taking care of - care for

5. go over - visit

6. find out - discover

7. come over - visit (the person being visited uses this)

8. eat out - eat at a restaurant instead of home

9. looking forward to - anticipate with pleasure

Task 4

I have never gotten along with my sister. She always talks back to our parents. Last summer I grew sick of it. I needed to take a break from her, or I would go crazy! I thought of a plan that would help. I decided to abandon my family once and for all...

Task 5

1.   I am putting on weight, I need to cut down on my chocolate eating!

2.   She looks up to her older brother.

194

3.   - *Do you want to go on a walk in the countryside today?*

   - *Sure, but we'll have to look out for rattlesnakes!*

4.   *Make sure of the situation before you act.*

5.   *When I think back on our marriage, I remember all the good parts.*

Phrasal Verbs with 'Take'

Mini-Dictionary & Exercise Worksheet for Students (Photocopiable)

Phrasal Verbs with 'take'

Here is a list with some examples of the most common phrasal verbs with 'take'. Use this glossary to complete exercises at the end of this chapter.

To be taken aback- Meaning: Surprise or shock. Example: *It took me aback when she asked such a personal question.*

Take after- Meaning: To have similar appearance, character or personality to an older family member. Example*: She takes after her father.*

Take against- Meaning: Stop liking someone; to become hostile toward. Example: *She took against Mary when she was promoted over her.*

Take apart- Meaning: Separate something into its parts. Example: *The mechanic took the car apart to find the problem.*

Take aside- Meaning: Get someone alone to talk to them. Example: *John was taken aside by the manager when he shouted at a customer. .*

Take away- Meaning: Remove something and put it in a different place. Example: *My dad took our plates away and came back with chocolate cake for dessert!*

Take away- Meaning: Remove something, either material or abstract, so that a person no longer has it. Example: *Jack's mum took his computer away until he improved at school.*

Take away- Meaning: Subtract or diminish something. Example: *If I have three oranges and I take away two, how many oranges do I have left? The answer is …. one.*

Take away- Meaning: Leave a memory or impression in one's mind that you think about later. Example*: I took away the impression that the manager did not get along with his players.*

Take away- Meaning: Force someone to leave a place and take him or her somewhere else. Example: *The police took the suspect to the station for questioning.*

Take away from- Meaning: Make something seem worse, not so good or less interesting. Example: *His behavior took away from the excitement of the party.*

Take back- Meaning: Retract something you said earlier. Example: *You are not selfish; I take it back, I'm sorry.*

Take back- Meaning: When something makes you remember some past event or time we say that it 'takes you back'. Example: *That film takes me back to when I was a kid at Christmas.*

Take back- Meaning: Start a relationship again with someone after you have split up. Example: *Jane has forgiven Aaron and taken him back despite his behavior.*

Take back- Meaning: Regain possession of something. Example: *I'm taking back my laptop because you are always using it without asking!*

Take back- Meaning: Return something to a shop for a refund or exchange. Example: *These shoes are too small, I'm going to have to take them back to the shop tomorrow.*

Take down- Meaning: Remove something from a wall or similar vertical surface to which it is fixed or handing position. Example: *She took down the photograph and replaced it with the framed picture.*

Take down- Meaning: Make notes, especially to record something spoken. Example: *If you have a pen, you should take down the most important points of the lecture.*

Take down- Meaning: Remove a temporary structure. Example: *When everything else is ready, we can take down the gazebo.*

Take down- Meaning: Lower an item of clothing without removing it. Example: *The nurse asked me to take down my trousers.*

Take for- Meaning. Think of or regard as. Example: *What do you take me for, a fool?*

Take for- Meaning: to get confused about what something or who someone is. Example: *Sorry, I took you for someone else, you look like a friend of mine.-*

Take for (also 'take in for', 'take for a ride', 'rip off' or 'do' someone)- Meaning: Defraud. Example: *Jane is very upset because the scammers took her for 500 pounds.*

Take in- Meaning: Shorten (a piece of clothing) or make it smaller. Example: *I asked the tailor to take the trousers in a bit around the leg.*

Take in- Meaning: Absorb information or understand the reality of that information

Example: *He was in shock after the incident, so it took him a while to take the news in.*

Take in- Meaning: Deceive, give a false impression. Example: *Everyone was taken in by his lies.*

Take it out on- Meaning: Unleash one's anger on [a person or thing other than the one that caused it]. Example: *Don't take it out on me just because you're in a bad mood.*

Take it upon oneself- Meaning: Assume personal responsibility for a task or action. Example: *She took it upon herself to ring him and ask him to come over.*

Take off- Meaning: To remove something, usually clothes or accessories. Example: *The doctor asked me to take off my shirt.*

Take off- Meaning: Imitate, often in a comical manner. Example: *John Kraven is a comedian who takes off all the famous people in my country.*

Take off- Meaning: When an aircraft leaves the ground and begins to fly; to ascend into the air. Example: *The helicopter took off at 6pm.*

Take off- Meaning: to become successful or grow. Example: *The project has really taken off this year, we are very excited.*

Take off- Meaning: to leave. Example: *We have to take off now or we are going to be late.*

Take on- Meaning: introduce, bring in or acquire. Example: *The truck took on 50 pallets in Southampton this morning.*

Take on- Meaning: employ, bring in. Example: *When the number of customers increased, we had to take on more staff.*

Take on- Meaning: Begin to have or exhibit physical traits. Example: *He took on the appearance of a criminal for the role in his new movie.*

Take on- Meaning: Take responsibility or burden. Example: *I'll take on the extra work if you can manage the project.*

Take on- Meaning: Attempt to fight or compete with. Example: *They took on the most notorious gang members in the city and they won.*

Take out-Meaning: Remove. Example: *Please take out the rubbish before the kitchen starts to smell!*

Take out- Meaning: Invite someone out socially, often for romantic reasons. Example: *Let me take you out for a drink*

Take over- Meaning: Adopt a responsibility or duty from someone else. Example: *He will take over the job permanently when the accountant retires.*

Take over- Meaning: Take control of something for someone temporarily. Example: *Can you take over driving for half an hour while I get some shut-eye (sleep)?*

Take over- Meaning: Buy the control of a business. Example: *Rola Cola PLC is planning to take over Punjabi MC Ltd this month.*

Take over- Meaning: Take control by conquest or invasion. Example: *Germany took over half of Europe leading up to WW2. (Note: "Lead up to" means "in the events which caused, and which came before")*

Take to- Meaning: Adapt to; to learn, grasp or master something. Example: *He took to gold instantly, he was a natural.* (Note: "a natural" means someone who has natural talent at something)

Take to- Meaning: to go into or move towards. Example: *As we drove through field, dozens of birds took to the air, scared by the noise of the car.*

Take up- Meaning: to start doing (an activity) regularly. Example: *I'm thinking of taking up tennis once a week.*

Take up- Meaning: to start to talk about an issue or problem with someone. Example: *I took my concerns up with the manager.*

Take up- Meaning: Occupy; to consume (space or time). Example: *The sofa takes up half the living room.*

Take up- Meaning: Accept a proposal or offer

Example:

John: *Next time you´re in town, I´ll buy you a beer.*

James: *I´ll take you up on that!*

Take through- Meaning: Explain in steps; give a tour of a place. Example: *Let me take you through the basics of how to cook Southern Fried Chicken*

Exercise 1

For each of the six questions choose the one correct answer. You might need to check the glossary above.

1. When his father retires, he's planning to take _____ his factory in Beijing.

a. off

b. after

c. up

d. over

2. Our plane took ___ 2 hours late!

a. over

b. up

c. off

d. after

3. Why do so many men take ___ golf when they retire?

a. over

b. off

c. up

d. after

4. Roberto gets angry a lot, he takes ___ his father.

a. over

b. off

c. in

d. after

5. When I heard she was pregnant, I couldn't take it ____ at first.

a. after

b. over

c. in

d. off

6. I was completely taken ___ when he told me he was working late at the office.

a. after

b. in

c. over

d. after

Exercise 2

1 Match each sentence beginning 1 - 10 with an appropriate ending a) – j).

1 She is very similar to her mother, whereas her sister takes

2 The new CEO is very serious, and we haven't really taken

3 I need to remember this lesson. I'll get a pen and paper and take

4 My feet are swollen. I think I'll take

5 This jumper is too big. I need to take

6 When my mum retired, I took

7 Michael's become inseparable from his bike since he took

8 You should get rid of this table. It's a small room and it takes

9 We have too much to do at work. We need to take

10 I thought I could manage this job, but I think I've taken

a) it back.

b) on more staff

c) on too much

d) up half the room.

e) up cycling.

f) off my shoes.

g) over the family business.

h) to her.

i) after her father.

j) down the most important parts.

Exercise 3

Now write the infinitive of each of the phrasal verbs with 'take' from exercise 2 next to its meaning below.

a) accept the responsibility for something _____

b) start a new hobby or activity _____

c) start to like or feel good about _____

d) to employ (give a job to) _____

e) remind or provoke memories _____

f) to become successful _____

g) make notes _____

h) to be similar in appearance or personality _____

i) take control of _____

j) occupy space or time _____

Answers:

Exercise 1

1:

a. 'Take off' usually refers to planes or clothes!

b. 'Take after' means 'similar to'.

c. 'Take up' means begin a sport or hobby.

d. Correct - He plans to 'take over' the factory – take control of it.

2:

a. 'Take over' usually means take control of.

b. 'Take up' means begin a sport or hobby.

c. Correct - The plane 'took off' 2 hours late is correct. It departed or left the ground.

d. 'Take after' means 'similar to'.

3:

a. 'Take over' usually means take control of.

b. 'Take off' usually refers to planes or clothes!

c. Correct - 'Take up' means begin a sport or hobby.

d. 'Take after' means 'similar to'.

4:

a. 'Take over' usually means take control of.

b. 'Take off' usually refers to planes or clothes!

c. 'Take in' means to try to understand something or to fool someone.

d. Correct - 'Take after' means 'similar to'. 'He takes after his father'.

5:

a. 'Take after' means 'similar to'.

b. 'Take over' usually means take control of.

c. Correct - Take in' means to try to understand something – often used in the

negative.

d. 'Take off' usually refers to planes or clothes!

6:

a. 'Take after' means 'similar to'.

b. Correct - 'Take in' means to be fooled by someone. 'I was taken in by his lies'

c. 'Take over' usually means take control of.

d. 'Take after' means 'similar to'.

Exercise 2

1 She is very similar to her mother, whereas her sister takes after her father.

2 The new CEO is very serious, and we haven't really taken to her.

3 I need to remember this lesson. I'll get a pen and paper and take

4 My feet are swollen. I think I'll take off my shoes.

5 This jumper is too big. I need to take it back.

6 When my mum retired, I took over the family business.

7 Michael's become inseparable from his bike since he took up cycling.

8 You should get rid of this table. It's a small room and it takes up half the room.

9 We have too much to do at work. We need to take on more staff.

10 I thought I could manage this job, but I think I've taken on too much.

Exercise 3

a) accept the responsibility for something – Take on

b) start a new hobby or activity – Take up

c) start to like or feel good about – Take to

d) to employ (give a job to) – Take on

e) remind or provoke memories – Take back

f) to become successful – Take off

g) make notes   - Take down

h) to be similar in appearance or personality- Take after

i) take control of- Take over

j) occupy space or time- Take up

CONVERSATION QUESTIONS: *TAKE*

Instructions: Hand out the conversation questions to students. Both students will have the same questions. They should ask and answer the questions, trying to make the conversation as natural as possible. The teacher can circulate and help students as needed.

STUDENT A

1. Who do you *take after* in your family?
2. What *takes up* most of your time?
3. When was the last time you really *took to* someone you had just met?
4. What activities would you like to *take up* in the future? Why?

....

STUDENT B

1. Who do you *take after* in your family?
2. What *takes up* most of your time?
3. When was the last time you really *took to* someone you had just met?
4. What activities would you like to *take up* in the future? Why?

PHRASAL VERBS WITH 'PUT'

Mini-Dictionary & Exercise Worksheet for Students (Photocopiable)

Phrasal Verbs with 'put'

Here is a list with some examples of the most common phrasal verbs with 'put'. Use this glossary to complete exercises at the end of this chapter.

Put out- Meaning: Extinguish a light or something which has fire. Example: *Put out your cigarette please, this is a no-smoking area.*

Put out- Meaning: Release or publish. Example: *We need to put out an email explaining the situation.*

Put (effort) into- Meaning: To try. Example: I put a lot of work into the presentation.

Put across- Meaning: Explain or communicate something clearly and understandably. Example: The way she put the message across was quite rude.

Put aside- Meaning: Save (money). Example: *I try to put a few quid aside every day for our summer holiday. (Note: "quid" is slang for British pounds)*

Put aside- Meaning: Ignore or intentionally disregard (something), temporarily or permanently. Example: *We need to put our differences aside.*

Put away- Meaning: put something somewhere organized or out of sight. Example: *When I tidy my room I put all my clothes away.*

Put away- Meaning: Consume in large quantities (food and drink). **Example**: *He put away 12 chicken wings, 2 steaks and a whole roast chicken.. What a beast!*

Put away- Meaning: Send to jail. Example: *They put her away for 2 years on weapons charges.*

Put back- Meaning: Return something to its original place. **Example**: She put the toys back in the cupboard.

Put back- Meaning: Postpone a meeting, event or appointment. Example: *The meeting has been put back to 2pm due to the storms.*

Put down- Meaning: Belittle, humiliate or demean. Example: *She's not very nice, she constantly puts her husband down.*

Put down- Meaning: Pay a deposit or initial installment. Example: *She put down a 2,000-euro deposit.*

Put down- Meaning: Eliminate or stop by force. Example: *Government security forces quickly put down the civil unrest.*

Put down- Meaning: Kill an animal because it is sick or suffering.. Example: *We had to put our dog down last month because he was too ill.*

Put down- Meaning: Write (something). Example: *Put down your name and address on this paper.*

Put down- Meaning: Finish a phone-call; to hang up. Example: *Don't put the phone down please, I want to apologize to you!*

Put down- Meaning: Add a name to a list. Example: *I've put myself down on the VIP list for the party. .*

Put down or Putting up- Meaning: Make prices, or taxes, lower or higher. Example: *The Chinese government are putting up the price of oil in order to stimulate the use of renewable energies.*

Put down- Meaning: Place a baby somewhere to sleep. **Example**: *I have just put Charley down so please be quiet!*

Put down (a book)- Meaning: Stop, temporarily or permanently, reading (a book). Example: *I can´t put this book down, it´s so interesting!*

Put down as- Meaning: Make assumptions about someone´s personality. **. Example**: *I put her down as an arrogant, materialistic snob, but she is actually very sweet.*

Put down for- Meaning: Put someone on a list of people who have offered to help or contribute to something. Example: *Put Jack down to help with the cleaning, he told me he wanted to do it.*

Put down to- Meaning: assume or come to the conclusion about the cause of a situation. Example: *We often put high crime rates down to high unemployment.*

214

Put on- Meaning: To fake or pretend. Example: *He puts on funny accents to make us laugh.*

Put on (clothes)- Meaning: To fit clothes on your body. Example: *It's really sunny, I need to put my hat on!*

Put on- Meaning: To blame someone else for something. Example: *You can't put that on me, it wasn't my fault!*

Put on (weight)- Meaning: To gain weight or fat. Example: *I have put on at least 2 stone over Christmas. I didn't stop eating!*

Put forward (a suggestion or idea)- Meaning: Propose for consideration. Example: *The CEO put forward new plans to reduce costs.*

Put forward- Meaning: Change the time in a time zone to a later time. Example: *I almost forgot that we have to put the clocks forward tomorrow by 1 hour.*

Put up with- Meaning: Tolerate. Example: *I'm too tired to put up with him, his attitude annoys me.*

Put up- Meaning: Offer accommodation for the night. Example: *My parents put us up while our house was being re-furbished.*

Put up- Meaning: raise. Example: *Put your hands up in the air like you just don't care!*

Put someone up to something- Meaning: manipulate someone or convince them to do something. Example: *Did Mary put you up to this? I told her I didn't want to talk about my problem.*

215

Put off- Meaning: Distract. Example: *Don´t try to put me off the game, that´s cheating!*

Put off- Meaning: Delay. Example: *We put off the show because of the rain.*

Put someone off something or someone- Meaning: Make someone stop liking something or someone. Example: *Her lack of a sense of humor put me off her, so I didn´t ask her out*

Exercise 1

Phrasal verbs with 'put'

Match each sentence beginning 1 - 12 with an appropriate ending a) – l).

1. It's raining quite heavily. You should put on
2. I didn´t recognize her when I saw her because she had put on
3. There's nothing good on TV. Why don´t we put on
4. She might need to move. Her landlady has put up
5. We need to put up new
6. Put your hand up
7. My parents offered to put
8. How do you put up
9. We had to put off the meeting
10. It snowed so heavily that it put us off
11. I could never concentrate at university, because all
12. We need to put out

a) us up for the weekend when we go to visit.

b) a lot of weight.

c) because the CEO was stuck in traffic.

d) with her constant moaning?

e) your new coat.

f) the fire before it spreads.

g) going out, so we watched a film instead.

h) the parties and the noise put me off.

i) her rent.

j) an online film?

k) curtains because the old ones have holes in them.

l) if you have any questions.

Exercise 2

Now decide which phrasal verb is needed in each sentence:

1. I can't ___ her anymore, she's driving me bonkers! *(Note: to drive someone bonkers means to drive him or her crazy- to annoy)*

Put on

Put back

Put up with

2. Please ___ the bread when you're finished using it.

Put back

Put on

Put down

3. Can you ___ the conference until Friday please?

Put up

Put off

Put down

4. She ___ all the time, but he's still married to her.

Puts him up

Puts him across

Puts him down

5. They ___ a new blog post every week. It's really good.

Put up with

Put down

Put out

6. I was trying to ___ my opinion but no one listened.

Put away

Put across

Put up with

Answers:

Exercise 1

It's raining quite heavily. You should put on your new coat.

I didn´t recognize her when I saw her because she had put on a lot of weight.

There's nothing good on TV. Why don´t we put on an online film?

She might need to move. Her landlady has put up her rent.

We need to put up new curtains because the old ones have holes in them.

Put your hand up if you have any questions.

My parents offered to put us up for the weekend when we go to visit.

How do you put up with her constant moaning?

We had to put off the meeting because the CEO was stuck in traffic.

It snowed so heavily that it put us off going out, so we watched a film instead.

I could never concentrate at university, because all the parties and the noise put me off.

We need to put out the fire before it spreads.

Exercise 2

1. I can't ___ her anymore, she's driving me bonkers! (Note: to drive someone bonkers means to drive him or her crazy- to annoy)

Put on

Put back

<u>Put up with</u>

2. Please ___ the bread when you're finished using it.

<u>Put back</u>

Put on

Put down

3. Can you ___ the conference until Friday please?

Put up

<u>Put off</u>

Put down

4. She ___ all the time, but he's still married to her.

Puts him up

221

Puts him across

<u>Puts him down</u>

5. They __ a new blog-post every week. It's really good.

Put up with

Put down

<u>Put out</u>

6. I was trying to __ my opinion but no one listened.

Put away

<u>Put across</u>

Put up with

CONVERSATION QUESTIONS: *PUT*

Instructions: Hand out the conversation questions to students. Both students will have the same questions. They should ask and answer the questions, trying to make the conversation as natural as possible. The teacher can circulate and help students as needed.

STUDENT A

1. What sort of thigs do you usually *put off* until the last minute?
2. What can people do to *put their ideas across* better in English?
3. What sort of things do you have to *put up with* that you don't like?
4. What was the name of the last book you couldn't *put down*?

....

STUDENT B

1. What sort of thigs do you usually *put off* until the last minute?
2. What can people do to *put their ideas across* better in English?
3. What sort of things do you have to *put up with* that you don't like?
4. What was the name of the last book you couldn't *put down*?

Phrasal Verbs with 'Get'

Mini-Dictionary & Exercise Worksheet for Students (Photocopiable)

Phrasal Verbs with 'get'

Here is a list with some examples of the most common phrasal verbs with 'get'. Use this glossary to complete exercises at the end of this chapter.

get across (separable) – to communicate clearly. Example: *The man was so stubborn that we couldn´t get the message across and change his mind.*

get ahead (intransitive - no object) – to make progress. **Example**: *She needs to work hard in life if she wishes to be successful.*

get along (get on) (intransitive) – to have a good relationship. Example: *I get along very well with my grandfather. We have similar personalities.*

get around (1)- (inseparable) – to avoid or to overcome a problem, a rule, or a challenge. **Example**: *Walter got around the rules by pretending he didn´t know about them.*

get around (2)- (intransitive - no object) – to go from place to place. **Example:** Since he lives in the city center, he gets around everywhere on foot.

get around to (3) – to finally do something. **Example:** *We finally got round to clearing the loft after three months!*

get at- (intransitive - no object) – to hint or to mean. Example: *What are you getting at? Can you be more specific and give me an example?*

get at– to reach so that you can take something. Example: *Can you pass me that bottle please? I can't get at it because I'm too short.*

get away- (intransitive - no object) – to escape. **Example:** *The prisoners got away through a hole in the wall.*

get away with something– to escape responsibility. **Example:** *We got away with not doing our homework because we told the teacher that our dog had eaten it.*

get back- (intransitive - no object) – to return. Example: *Jeremy always gets back late from the office. He has a very intense job.*

get by- (intransitive - no object) – to survive. **Example:** *When we were young my family had no money, but we got by.*

get down (to)- (intransitive - no object) – to concentrate or focus on a task. . Example: *Let's get down to business. We need to find a solution to the supply problem. .*

get down (1)- (separable) – to discourage. **Example:** *Don't let the rain get you down!*

get down (2)- (separable) – to put in writing- Example: *Please Bob, can you get the minutes down during the meeting?*

get in- (intransitive - no object) – to arrive. **Example**: *The bus got in an hour early because of the mistake in the timetable.*

get off (1)- (inseparable) – to leave. Example: *I forgot my hat when I got off the train.*

get off (2)- (intransitive - no object) – to receive lesser punishment. **Example**: *He crashed his car into a shop window because he was on his phone, but he got off with just a small fine and some community service.*

get off (3)- (separable) – to interrupt. **Example**: *We have the day off today because of the floods. We don't have to go to work!*

get out (1)- (intransitive - no object) – to spread. **Example**: *Word gets out quickly in our small village, so everyone knew Michael was planning on proposing to Jess.*

get out (of) (2)- (inseparable) – to escape. Example: *Joe always has an excuse and gets out of cleaning the car.*

get out (of) (3)- (inseparable) – to leave. **Example**: *Let's get out of here.. I'm hot and tired!*

get over- (inseparable) – to recover. Example: *It took Jill some time to get over her divorce.*

get rid of- (inseparable) – dispose of something or dismiss someone. **Example**: *Please get rid of that old bike. It's so dirty*

get through (1)- (inseparable) – to finish. **Example**: *We need to get through at least 6 pages of material in today's lesson.*

get through (2)- (inseparable) – to communicate a message effectively. **Example**: *We need to get through to him before he does something stupid, but he doesn't listen.*

get to (1)- (inseparable) – to annoy. **Example**: *His comments got to me!*

get to (2)- (inseparable) – to arrive . **Example**: *What time will you get to the station?*

get together- (intransitive - no object) – to meet up with someone . Example: *They got together for a drink and 6 months later they were married!*

get up- (intransitive - no object) – wake up and get out of bed . **Example**: *My new job starts at 8 am so I have to get up at 6 o'clock.*

get up to– to do . **Example**: *What did you get up to yesterday?*

Exercise 1

Read the sentences below. Underline the phrasal verbs and try to work out the meaning from the context. Then complete the gaps below each sentence using one of the following meanings.

to communicate a message effectively

to reach so that you can take something

to communicate clearly

to escape responsibility

to avoid or to overcome a problem, a rule, or a challenge

to escape

to discourage

to recover

1) They realized it would be a difficult challenge, but after a lot of hard work they got around it.

Phrasal Verb: ....

Meaning: ....

2) I can never get at the top shelf in the supermarket, so I always have to ask for help. I wish I were taller.

Phrasal Verb: ....

Meaning: ....

3) After Jim had made several unsuccessful attempts to get through to Sally, he realized she wasn't listening, so he went home.

Phrasal Verb: ....

Meaning: ....

4) Albert managed to get away from the meeting early for Mary's birthday.

Phrasal Verb: ....

Meaning: ....

5) My girlfriend left me last month and I felt very sad, but I've got over it now.

Phrasal Verb: ....

Meaning: ....

6) I don't like sad films, they really get me down.

Phrasal Verb: ....

229

Meaning: ....

7) Jason is a good presenter who always gets his message across.

Phrasal Verb: ....

Meaning: ....

8) The police didn´t catch the thief, so he got away with it.

Phrasal Verb: ....

Meaning: ....

Answers:

1) They realized it would be a difficult challenge, but after a lot of hard work they got around it.

get around

to avoid or to overcome a problem, a rule, or a challenge

2) I can never get at the top shelf in the supermarket, so I always have to ask for help. I wish I were taller.

get at

to reach so that you can take something

3) After Jim had made several unsuccessful attempts to get through to Sally, he realized she wasn't listening, so he went home.

get through–

to communicate a message effectively

4) Albert managed to get away from the meeting early for Mary's birthday.

get away-

to escape

231

5) My girlfriend left me last month and I felt very sad, but I've got over it now.

get over-

to recover

6) I don't like sad films, they really get me down.

get down

to discourage

7) Jason is a good presenter who always gets his message across.

get across–

to communicate clearly

8) The police didn't catch the thief, so he got away with it.

get away with–

to escape responsibility

CONVERSATION QUESTIONS: *GET*

Instructions: Hand out the conversation questions to students. Both students will have the same questions. They should ask and answer the questions, trying to make the conversation as natural as possible. The teacher can circulate and help students as needed.

STUDENT A

1. What advice would you give to people who want to *get ahead* in their career?
2. What's the best way to *get around* your home town?
3. Did you used to *get away with* mischief as a child? Explain.
4. What's the best way to *get your message across* in a presentation?

....

STUDENT B

1. What advice would you give to people who want to *get ahead* in their career?
2. What's the best way to *get around* your home town?
3. Did you used to *get away with* mischief as a child? Explain.
4. What's the best way to *get your message across* in a presentation?

Phrasal Verbs with 'Come'

Mini-Dictionary & Exercise Worksheet for Students (Photocopiable)

Phrasal Verbs with 'come'

Here is a list with some examples of the most common phrasal verbs with 'come'. Use this glossary to complete exercises at the end of this chapter.

come across (1)- (inseparable) – to find. **Example**: *I came across a very interesting book while browsing the second-hand bookshops in Manchester.*

come across (2)- (inseparable) – to give the impression or appearance. **Example**: *He came across quite arrogant at first, but he was a nice guy.*

come along (1)- (intransitive - no object) – to progress. **Example**: *How is her assignment coming along?*

come along (2)- (intransitive - no object) – to casually attend or appear somewhere. **Example**: *When Jenny came along after work, Robbie left because he was still angry with her.*

come around- (intransitive - no object) – to change opinions. **Example**: *After hours of arguing he finally came round (he agreed with me)*

234

come back (1)- (inseparable) -- to return. **Example**: *Madison comes back from London tomorrow. We need to pick her up from the airport at 2.*

come back (2)- (inseparable) -- to remember- when a memory returns because of something you see, hear or feel. **Example**: *It all came back to me when I saw the ring. I'd forgotten everything, but now I remember.*

come by- (inseparable) – to get or obtain. **Example**: *I came by this watch when I was walking along the beach and found it.*

come down (with)- (inseparable) – to become ill. Example: *Maybe you should go to the doctor's. This is the third time you've come down with a cold this month.*

come from- (inseparable) -- to originate. **Example**: *Madison comes from a wealthy family. Jack comes from England.*

come in- (inseparable) -- to finish. **Example**: *Madison came in last in the race, but she enjoyed herself.*

come into- (inseparable) -- to acquire. **Example**: *Madison came into money when she was 21, after her parents suddenly died.*

come off (1)- (intransitive - no object) – to give the impression. **Example**: *Jack comes off as a hard person, but in fact he is quite caring.*

come off (2)- (intransitive - no object) – to stop taking a drug or medication. **Example**: *Mick is coming off drugs, he has a serious addiction.*

come on- (intransitive - no object) – to give the impression. **Example**: *Jack comes on as a hard person, but in fact he is quite caring.*

come on- (intransitive - no object) – to start to work (water, electricity etc..). **Example**: *The electricity came back on two hours after the power cut.*

come out- (intransitive - no object) – to be revealed or to reveal information. **Example**: *The player's past came out when his old friends spoke to the press.*

come over- (intransitive - no object) – to visit causally or spontaneously. **Example**: *Come over for dinner tonight, we´re having a Sunday roast!*

come through- (intransitive - no object) – to do what is expected. **Example**: *William came through only after Wanda begged him for three days to get the tickets for the game.*

come to- (inseparable) – to total (counting money). **Example**: *The restaurant bill comes to 150 dollars*

come up- (intransitive - no object) – to be mentioned in conversation. Example: *The topic of his money problems came up during the conversation.*

come up with- (inseparable) – to invent or think about something new. **Example**: *Joe came up with a very good idea for the marketing campaign.*

come upon- (inseparable) – to discover by accident- Example: *While cleaning the house, we came upon an amazing picture from the 19th century.*

236

Exercise 1:

Write the correct preposition to make meaningful sentences.

1. Mary comes .... Ireland and she was born in Dublin.

2. Jason came .... last in the marathon.

3. He came............... home quite late, but he had a good reason.

4. I came .... some old friends at the party.

5. The price of oil is coming ...., so demand will go up.

6. She is trying to come .... the medication but she has to do it gradually.

7. They came .... to Coventry last Christmas, so we've got to go over to theirs this year.

Exercise 2:

Complete the phrasal verb for each sentence. Use the glossary in this unit if you need to.

1. I .... a lot of money when I turned 18 because I inherited it from my grandparents.

2. Now I remember! It´s all .... to me.

3. The truth .... when one of the witnesses spoke to reporters and it was published in the press.

4. We need to .... with some creative ideas for the new story. It should be an action thriller with a strong main character.

Answers:

Exercise 1

1. *Mary comes from Ireland and she was born in Dublin.*
2. *Jason came in last in the marathon.*
3. *He came back home quite late, but he had a good reason.*
4. *I came across some old friends at the party.*
5. *The price of oil is coming down, so demand will go up.*
6. *She is trying to come off the medication, but she has to do it gradually.*
7. *They came over to Coventry last Christmas, so we've got to go over to theirs this year.*

Exercise 2

1. *Came into*
2. *Coming back*
3. *Came out*
4. *Come up*

CONVERSATION QUESTIONS: *COME*

Instructions: Hand out the conversation questions to students. They should ask and answer the questions, trying to make the conversation as natural as possible. The teacher can circulate and help students as needed.

STUDENT A

1. Think of something you found in the past. Explain how you *came across* it.
2. Think of a time when someone (e.g. a friend or family member) *came through* for you. Explain the situation.
3. Can you think of any famous people who *come off* as shallow and self-absorbed? Why do you think they *come off* like this?
4. When was the last time you *came down* with a cold? Describe the situation and how you felt.

....

STUDENT B

1. Think of something you found in the past. Explain how you *came across* it.
2. Think of a time when someone (e.g. a friend or family member) *came through* for you. Explain the situation.
3. Can you think of any famous people who *come off* as shallow and self-absorbed? Why do you think they *come off* like this?
4. When was the last time you *came down* with a cold? Describe the situation and how you felt.

BONUS CHAPTER: FORMAL VS INFORMAL LANGUAGE

SIX Quick Rules of Formal VS Informal:

1. In formal English (particularly in the UK), we tend to understate our feelings and would say *I was rather disappointed,* or *I was somewhat surprised* instead of saying how we really felt.

2. For the same reason, we do not usually use exclamation marks when we are writing formally.

3. In formal situations, we often use the passive to emphasize the action when the person is of less importance.

4. We avoid contractions in formal letters.

5. We use formal equivalence of idiomatic language and phrasal verbs

6. Particular sentence structures can be used to create a formal tone. Inversion is one example of this "Although we were offered an alternative dish, when it was delivered to the table it was cold again".

Formal VS Informal Language List:

It is vital that you can distinguish between formal and informal language in English, not only for this exam, but also for life in general. Writing a letter or email to a friend is obviously not the same as writing a letter of recommendation for a friend who has applied for a job.

Here are some examples of formal and informal words with the same meaning,

FORMAL	INFORMAL
to depart	go
to retain	keep
to cease	stop
to function	work
to demonstrate	show
to reside	live
deficiency	lack
perspiration	sweat
inexpensive	cheap
require	need
subsequently	next / later
immature, infantile	childish
sufficient	enough
further	more (information)
assist, aid	to help
liberate	to free
obtain	to get
to desire	want
request	to ask for
therefore	so
to seek	look for

LINKING WORDS

LINKING MARKERS

Openers		Conjunctions	
Co-ordinating		**Subordinating**	
ADDITION	In addition [to NP], ...	...and ...	, who...
	Moreover, ...	not only ...,	, which...
	Also, ...	but also ...	, where...
	Apart from [NP], ...		, when...
	Furthermore, ...		
CONTRAST	However, ...	... but ...	although...
	Nevertheless, ...	...(and) yet...	whereas...
	On the other hand, ...		while...
	In contrast, ...		in spite of the fact tha
	In spite of [NP], ...		despite the fact that...
	Despite [NP], ...		
CAUSE/	So...	...(and) so...	so...
EFFECT	As a result...	...(and) hence...	so that...
	Consequently...		because...
	Therefore...		due to the fact that...
	Thus...		
	Hence...		
	For this reason...		
	Because of [NP],...		
POSITIVE	In that case,...	...and...	if...
CONDITION	If so,...	...and (then)...	as/so long as...

244

Note: [NP] = Noun Phrase, which may include a noun, or a verbal noun (-ing form):

e.g. Instead of <u>complaints</u>, it would be better to offer advice

Instead of <u>complaining,</u>

Exercise 1

Rewrite the information below in 3 or 4 sentences. You must decide how the ideas are logically related and then use a marker or conjunction (coordinating or subordinating) to match your meaning.

Learning French is not easy. Many people would argue that learning Spanish is harder.

French and English share a lot of similarities in their vocabulary. French and Spanish both have different articles for masculine and feminine nouns. You have to change the endings of adjectives to match the nouns. This is hard for speakers of English. English does not use adjective endings.

Most people believe that speaking English helps you to start learning French and Spanish. When you have passed the basic stages, English is less helpful. At an advanced level of Spanish and French, knowing English is arguably not very helpful.

Answers:

Learning French is not easy, but many people would argue that learning Spanish is harder, because French and English share a lot of similarities in their vocabulary. Nevertheless, French and Spanish both have different articles for masculine and feminine nouns. Therefore, you have to change the endings of adjectives to match the nouns, which is hard for speakers of English since English does not use adjective endings. Most people believe that speaking English helps you to start learning French and Spanish but when you have passed the basic stages, English is less helpful and at an advanced level of Spanish and French, knowing English is arguably not very helpful.

Student Handout: *How to Learn Thousands of Words in English in Only 6 Months*

Do you spend a lot of time and effort in learning vocabulary but still find difficulty using it when required? Have you spent a lot of time memorizing vocabulary words but forget them when you need them the most? Don't worry if you answered a big resounding "YES" to any of these questions because you are not alone. There are a number of useful tools, methods, and exercises which will have you not only remembering, but using your extended vocabulary with minimal effort. Let's get started!

Use Mnemonic Devices

What are mnemonic devices? Well they include a variety of techniques and methods that help remember or recall information.

FANBOYS

For example, many students often need to recall the conjunctions used in English grammar. Remembering FANBOYS is a good tool to recall these words (For, And, Nor, But, Or, Yet, So). The best part of this is you can use your creativity to make it interesting and different. You could create a song out of the words, similar to what many children do when they learn names of countries and capitals. Finding some words that rhyme together would give your song some rhythm, so get creative and don't be afraid to try something a bit silly. Silly is good because it helps the brain remember.

Tongue twisters

Tongue twisters are a fun way of practicing sounds, and this repetition of sounds creates another type of rhythm: *Silly Sally sat by the seashore collecting seashells.*

This can be done with words that begin with the same sound or even have similar sounds within or at the end of a word. It can create an interesting beat or jingle which helps you remember easily and quickly.

Teach it to the mirror!

One of the best and easiest ways to remember anything is to teach someone else. If you can't teach someone else, then teach yourself in the mirror!

Share your knowledge. In order to teach vocabulary to someone else, you need to have a good grasp of the word and the many contexts in which it is used. In fact, if you refer to a dictionary you may find that there are multiple definitions related to the word itself. Before teaching, it's important to study and thoroughly understand the word first. Look for sentences that contain that word, so you can understand how it can be used with other words for meaning. Practice making your own sentences as well. Encourage the "student" to ask questions for understanding and clarity.

248

Make it a part of your daily routine

Now it's important to use what you have learned. As the saying goes: "If you don't use it, you lose it." The first step here is to look for ways to use the new words.

Notecards or post-it notes

Notecards or post-it notes are useful as they are handy. You can stick post-its anywhere as a reminder. Just write the name, short definition, or even a sentence as an example. Here's what your notecard could look like:

Impart: to make known

Synonyms: tell, disclose

Sentence: Teachers impart knowledge to their students.

Learn Suffixes

Suffixes are word endings that may change a word's meaning. They can be used to change a word so that it maintains the rules of grammar. Consider the following sentences

It is a tradition in Chinese culture to eat using chopsticks.

The older generation is more traditional than today's youth.

The wedding ceremony is traditionally conducted by a priest.

249

Learning suffixes and how they change words is a useful tool. With the suffix -ally, as in "traditionally", it is understood that we are using an adverb describing an action. The –tion in "tradition" makes it a noun, so it's often placed at the beginning of a sentence. Understanding placement of words will help you make sure sentences are grammatically correct.

Read, Read, and Read!

Today's fast paced lifestyle makes it challenging, if not impossible, to make the time to read. However, tor increasing English vocabulary, it's absolutely essential. Read what you enjoy reading in your own language but read it in English! If you like music, read about music, if you like business, read business!

The 30-minute Rule

The 30-minute Rule states that thirty minutes of pleasurable reading every day will lead to amazing results in your level of English over time. 'Thirty-minute readers', people who read for fun for at least 30 minutes per day, tend to have a vast vocabulary. Furthermore, several studies have suggested that the health benefits can be considerable: living longer, increasing IQ, and reducing stress among other perks. Over time, reading regularly can also increase vocabulary and make it easier to utilize these words in practical and functional situations.

Don't worry if you can't find the time in a busy lifestyle to pick up a book to read.

Look for friends or colleagues who enjoy reading. Often times, interacting with bookworms or avid readers will help you pick up vocabulary or new expressions from them. Don't hesitate to ask about anything that is unfamiliar.

Read Newspapers

A newspaper is a very valuable tool that has a wealth of information at your fingertips. Whether it's the paper version or the electronic version, it doesn't matter. Newspapers are a tool which will spark curiosity and encourage you to read more about a variety of topics.

Spend time interacting with expert professionals in various fields if you can.

That doesn't mean you need to spend time at colleges or universities. Expand your field of awareness and interest to connect to those outside your circle of friends and colleagues. You can join various chat forums or groups in social media. Learn new vocabulary and subjects. You will definitely see the difference.

Download a dictionary app

Anyone who wants to improve their vocabulary really must download an app to their phone. It's not at all practical to lug around a dictionary. A dictionary app on a smartphone can be accessed quickly. Also, being familiar with some online tools that give sentence examples using the words in
251

different contexts is extremely useful. Remember that words fit together in sentences based on their meaning, so it's important to always understand the context or surrounding words so that the sentence or expression makes sense.

Record sentences and structures in your notebook, never single words

NEVER write a single word followed by a definition in your notebook! Always add an example sentence and pay attention to the original sentence where you saw this word. English words can often change meanings depending on the prepositions they go with or the type of sentence they are in.

For example:

He was turned away at the door because he was wearing trainers.

Meaning: He was rejected

He turned away when I tried to speak to him because he was very angry.

Meaning: He looked the other way or turned his head towards a different direction so he didn't have to look at me.

BONUS. FREE WEBSITES FOR ENGLISH PRACTICE

Reading

Links	Descriptions / Instructions
www.breakingnewsenglish.com/	News articles. Full lesson plans, including speaking and listening. GREAT EXERCISES! DO THE LESSON WITH A PARTNER!
http://esl.about.com/od	Various articles and resources with activities. Under **Categories** choose **Advanced English**. Under **Subtopics** choose **Advanced Reading Skills**. Select one of the **Articles &**

Resources	that interests you.
www.5minuteenglish.com/reading.htm	International Women's Day • Night Study in Korea
www.bbc.co.uk	The news in English. NO EXERCISES.
www.cnn.com/	The news in English. NO EXERCISES.

Grammar

Links	Descriptions / Instructions

254

www.englishlearner.com/tests/test.html	Various grammar and vocabulary exercises. Do **Upper Intermediate** and **Advanced** sections.

Listening

Links	Descriptions / Instructions
www.elllo.org/	Listen to the **Audio Archives (001-751+)** and answer the questions.
www.elllo.org/english/Points.htm	Short lectures with test-type questions.
www.esl-lab.com/	Listen to conversations from the **Difficult** section of the **General Listening Quizzes**. Listen to recordings from the **Medium** and **Difficult**

255

sections of the **Listening Quizzes for Academic Purposes** (EXAM-TYPE QUESTIONS).

Take dictation from the Upper-Intermediate and Advanced listening.

www.dictationsonline.com/

Includes punctuation vocabulary.

YOU NEED A PEN AND SOME PAPER.

Research and Writing

Links	Descriptions / Instructions
https://www.flo-joe.co.uk	Some good examples of writing corrections although be careful with errors on the

	website and inaccurate questions.
www.plainenglish.co.uk/proofreading.pdf	Proofreading – 10 ways to make your writing better.

Study Skills

Links	Descriptions / Instructions
www.how-to-study.com	Tips on studying effectively.

Pronunciation

Links	Descriptions / Instructions
www.shiporsheep.com/	Hear and practice similar sounds.
www.fonetiks.org/engsou5.html	Hear and practice similar consonants.
www.fonetiks.org/nameseng.html	Hear and practice English names.
www.fonetiks.org/difficult.html	Hear and practice difficult words.

www.howjsay.com/	A pronunciation dictionary.
www.spokenenglish.org/	Hear the pronunciation of various English grammar points.
www.foniks.org	Hear and practice sounds.

ADVANCED SPEAKING PHRASES (STUDENT HANDOUT)

Likes/dislikes	Opinion
I'm into... I'm a keen/avid (surfer) I'm keen on/fond of (surfing) I (go surfing) to unwind, to escape the stresses and strains of my day to day life. I like nothing more than (to go surfing) I'm itching to try/go.... (I really want to)	As far as I'm concerned, As I see it, From my point of view, In my humble opinion, I'd say that...
Comparing/contrasting	**Describing pictures**
Both pictures show... In this picture they look as though they are.... Whereas/while in this picture... In contrast On the other hand	The first thing that strikes me about this picture is... The thing that really jumps out of this picture is... In this picture it looks as if/though they are... They could/might/may be... They could/might/may have just... I'm pretty sure that they're feeling... I'd guess that they are...
Agreeing	**Disagreeing**
We see eye to eye. Yeah, I'd go along with that. Absolutely!	We don't see eye to eye. I take your point but... I tend to disagree with

You took the words right out of my mouth.	you there.
I couldn't agree more.	That's not always the case
You have a point there.	I beg to differ
I'm with you 100% on this one.	Isn't it more a case of...

Starting to make a conclusion	**Asking for opinion**
Let's get down to the nitty gritty.	What's your take on....?
The bottom line is we have to choose one...	Where do you stand on....?
It's a tough one, I'm torn between ... and	In my opinion...., would you go along with that?
Shall we go with ....?	What are your thoughts on this?

Personalizing	**Impressive structures**
Speaking from personal experience,...	Another point I'd like to add about ... is...
For me personally,..	It's also worth bearing in mind that...
This is a topic that is particularly close to my heart...	Coming back to what (Javi) was saying about .... I'd also like to point out that...
It's funny I was just thinking about this the other day.	I think it's important not to forget that...
My gut/initial reaction is...	The vast majority of people tend to think that...
If I were to choose one of these situations (part 2 pictures), I'd go with... because...	At the end of the day...
	When all's said and done...

Tips	**Asking for repetition**
Eye-contact	I beg your pardon, I didn't catch that.
Active listening	Sorry would you mind
Open body language	

Speak up Don't dominate	repeating that? Could you repeat the question please?

SECTION 4: ESL GAMES FOR ADULTS & TEENS

These ESL games and instant conversation worksheets can be adapted to suit any level, objective and age as warmers, introductions, review activities or fillers to provide language practice and opportunities for feedback. They have been tried and tested in ESL classrooms all over the world with great success.

Whether you're teaching children, teens or adults, knowing some good classroom activities is a must for any TESOL teacher. However interesting your lessons are, there will always be a point where students get bored of writing and listening - so having something prepared which will get them talking, laughing and even moving around will help them to stay engaged. Informal exercises are also an important way to get students comfortable with speaking and listening and can help to put vocabulary and grammar into a practical context.

While planned activities are important, it's also always worth having a few quick and easy games in mind in case you have time left over at the end of a lesson - so from quick games to creative projects, here are some of the best activities suitable for students at every level.

GAME 1

Level: Any

Good for: Vocabulary review / Quick end of lesson activities

Preparation:

Write out a list of familiar or recently-learned vocabulary on to pieces of paper - topics like professions, weather, food, actions, sports and animals are always good.

Split the class into two teams.

Activity:

Teams take it in turns to send student up to the whiteboard, where they are given a paper with one of the words on it. They then have 30 seconds to draw a picture of what they've read, while the rest of their team guesses what it is.

Rules:

If a team guesses the word in time, they get a point. The first team to set number of points wins.

You can also play this game with actions rather than drawings - so the student has to mime the word without speaking, writing, or making any sound.

GAME 2

Level: Any

Good for: Spelling review / Quick end of lesson activities

Preparation:

Divide the class into two teams and choose a word from recently learned vocabulary. Draw out a hangman game on the board.

Activity:

The teams take it in turns to guess a letter. Correct letters go into their blank spaces, while wrong guesses add a new part to the hanged man.

Rules:

The teams take it in turns until one guesses the word correctly and wins a point - in later rounds, you can also allow a student to choose the word for their opposing team to guess.

If all of the parts of the hanged man are drawn before a team can guess the word, no points are given.

GAME 3

Level: Any

Good for: Vocabulary review / End of lesson activities

Preparation:

Split the class into two teams and draw a tic tac toe grid on the board, with the squares numbered one to nine. Prepare up to 20 review questions or picture cards.

Activity:

Teams take it in turns to choose a number from the square of their choice. They are then asked the corresponding question or shown the picture card. If they correctly name the picture or get the question right, they can claim the square - if they get it wrong, the square remains free, and the other team can claim it by answering a different question correctly.

Rules:

The goal is for one team to claim three squares in a line - either vertically, diagonally, or horizontally.

GAME 4

Level: Any

Good for: Icebreakers

Preparation:

A toilet paper roll is passed around the classroom, and every student takes at least three squares.

Activity:

Once everyone has taken some, they have to count how many squares they have, and then tell the class one fact about themselves for each square of toilet paper they are holding - in English, of course! The activity of handing around the toilet roll, especially when students don't know the rules of the game, is a great way to get everyone focused and excited at the start of a new term.

If students are struggling to come up with statements, do some practice as a group, reviewing good examples. Complexity can vary depending on the level of the class.

GAME 5

Level: Any

Good for: Vocabulary review / End of lesson Activities

Preparation:

Announce a topic for vocabulary review and choose one
student to keep time and another to count how many correct
answers are given. Then choose three to five students to
leave the classroom and wait outside.

Activity:

Ask one of the students to come back into the classroom.
They then have 20 seconds to list as many words as they can
on the chosen topic. Once they're finished, invite in the next
student, and so on. The one who comes up with the most
words wins - repetition and made up words don't count!

Rules:

You can play as many rounds as you like, choosing a new
topic and selecting new students each time. It's also helpful
to invite the rest of the class to name any words they think
the other students missed at the end of each round.

GAME 6

Level: Any

Good for: Vocabulary review / Longer Activities

Preparation:

Students form groups of four or five - each group being one Ship. They then need to choose a Ship name - encourage them to think of animals, colors, countries, or movie stars that they like.

Each group then has to elect a Shooter and a Captain. The Captain's job is to remember the name of their own Ship. They will have to answer if another team calls out their name. The Shooter has to remember the name of the other Ships in the classroom.

Once the teams are formed, all of the Captains form a circle, with their other crew members in a line behind them, and the Shooter at the back.

Next, tell the students the topic of the vocabulary review - this can be anything from items of clothing to irregular verbs depending on the ability level of the class. The game works best when the subject matter has a lot of vocabulary for students to choose from.

Each Ship then has two minutes to think of as many words as possible and memorize them.

Activity:

Choose a team to start and call out their Ship's name. The Captain of the ship must then say one of the words from the chosen topic. For example, if the topic is items of clothing, they might say 'SCARF'. The student next in line behind the Captain then says another word, such as 'SHIRT', and the person behind them does the same - and so on until they reach the Shooter.

Rather than saying another vocabulary word, the Shooter instead chooses another Ship, and calls out their name. That Ship then has to do exactly the same thing - working back from the Captain from the Shooter.

Rules:

Shooters can't name their own Ship or choose one that's already been called.

Words can't be repeated, and everyone has to come up with a new word within three seconds. If a group takes too long, can't think of a new word or repeats one, or if a Shooter calls the name of a Ship that has already has a turn, their Ship has 'sunk'

When a Ship sinks, its crew (including the Captain and Shooter) goes to join another one.

Once every Ship has had a turn, the round is over. For the next round, choose another topic and carry on -, with the groups getting bigger as more Ships sink. The last Ship that hasn't sunk is the winner.

GAME 7

Level: Easy / Medium

Good for: Spelling review / Quick end of lesson activities

Preparation:

Write out a jumble of nine letters on the board - for example
H F O H R K S T I. Make sure there is a mix of vowels and
consonants. You can prepare the letters in advance if you
want to include specific vocabulary.

Activity:

Give students 30 seconds to write down as many words as
they can make out of the nine letters. So, in this case, they
might list 'hit', 'shirt', 'skirt', 'fork', and so on.

Rules:

Words must all be in English and spelled correctly! The
student with the most words is the winner.

GAME 8

Level: Easy / Medium

Good for: End of lesson activities

Preparation:

Every student is given a piece of paper, and one is selected to go first.

Activity:

The selected student starts describing a person without using their name, and all of the other students draw them on their paper. Once the description is finished, the students share their drawings.

Rules:

The person can be real - a celebrity or fictional character - or completely made up, although it's more fun if it's someone that everyone knows.

The game can be adapted to be about animals - or can be used to encourage students to draw a 'monster' by coming up with fantastical descriptions. It can also be used to practice

274

questions and answers - by inviting students to ask questions about what the person or animal looks like.

GAME 9

Level: Easy / Medium

Good for: Vocabulary review

Preparation:

Choose an area of vocabulary to review and write out a
selection of words on small pieces of paper. For this game,
the class will be split into two teams, and each will be given
an identical set of words - so make two copies of every word
and make them into two identical piles. To ensure that
everyone can take part, make sure you have enough words
for the whole class to play - and don't forget to keep a record
of the words for yourself as well!

Activity:

Divide the class into two teams and invite them to come up
with team names. Give both teams an identical bundle of
papers and get them to share them out until every student
has one piece of paper with a review word on it.

Call out one of the vocabulary words. One student from each
team should have that word on their piece of paper. They
then run to the whiteboard and write a sentence containing
that word.

Rules:

The fastest student is the winner - however, if a sentence isn't readable, doesn't make sense, or isn't spelled correctly, they are disqualified.

GAME 10

Level: Easy / Medium

Good for: Icebreakers / Conversation practice

Preparation:

Give each student a piece of paper and split them into teams of two. Before starting, review some 'getting to know you' questions - for example, 'How many brothers and sisters do you have?', 'What subject do you like best and why?', or 'What's your favorite movie'. Questions can be more or less complex depending on the ability level of the class.

Activity:

In their pairs, students ask each other five or six questions. They can note down their partner's answers on their paper if they like. Both people should have the chance to answer.

After everyone has finished, all of the students change partners, and tell their new partner about the person they just spoke to, using the information they just learned.

Once everyone has shared with their second partner, students stand up one by one and tell the rest of the class about the student they just learned about.

To make this game more listening-focused, you can take away the papers - so students only pass on what they remember. In this version, you can also get the rest of the class to guess who a student is describing at the end.

GAME 11

Level: Easy / Medium

Good for: Vocabulary Review / Big Classes

Preparation:

Give each student a piece of paper with category names across the top or get them to make their own (though this may take time). The categories can be customized to suit the vocabulary you've studied, but options such as Places, Animals, Activities, Objects, Fruit and Vegetables, Clothes etc. all work well. There should also be a Total column at the end.

Activity:

One student starts saying the alphabet out loud, from A to Z, until you shout 'STOP' at a random letter.

All of the students then have to write a word in each category, starting with that letter. So, if it was 'L', they might write Los Angeles, Llama, Listening, Lightbulb, Lemon and Leggings.

Rules:

The first student to write a word in every column shout 'STOP!' and everyone has to put their pens down.

280

Students then exchange their sheets, and everyone shares the words they chose. Write a list of them on the board - at the end, any words that were added by more than three students are worth 10 points. Words that were only chosen by two students get 20 points. Words that only one person picked get 50 points. Of course, all words have to be spelled correctly and fit in their category!

Students then add up their neighbor's points, and the one with the most wins the round.

This game can alternatively be played with a timer - so students have one or two minutes to put as many words as they can in every category. In this version there are no points - the student with the most correct words wins.

GAME 12

Level: Easy / Medium

Good for: Conversation practice

Preparation:

Start off by talking about vocabulary you've recently studied. Ask students who they think would use it, and why. For example, if they have been learning about weather, it might be people who are going on holiday, or who want to do an outdoor activity. Think about what other questions might be part of the same conversation - for example, what clothes you should wear.

Get two students to read out a prep-prepared sample conversation between two people on a relevant topic - for example:

TOM

Where are you going on holiday?

MARY

I'm going to Thailand.

282

TOM

What is the weather like there?

MARY

It's very hot and sunny, and it rains a lot in monsoon season.

TOM

You'll need to take an umbrella!

Then split the class into pairs.

Activity:

Instruct the pairs to each write a new conversation using
your reviewed vocabulary. For more advanced students, you
can set a minimum number of lines or ask them to
incorporate multiple topics.

Then choose some of the students to perform their
conversations to the rest of the class.

GAME 13

Level: Medium

Good for: Conversation practice / End of lesson activity

Preparation:

Make sure to go over question and answer formats with the class before starting.

Activity:

Choose an item or activity, then go around the class inviting students to ask yes or no questions to try and guess what it is - such as 'is it heavy?', 'does it make a sound?', 'do you do it at school?'', or 'is it fun?'. They are allowed to ask a maximum of 20 questions, plus three guesses at the end.

Rules:

The first student to correctly guess the item or action gets to choose the next word and answer questions from the rest of the class.

This game can also be played by splitting the class into pairs - with one person in every pair choosing the word, and the other asking the questions. If doing it this way, give them around five minutes to play one round, then switch. For lower ability classes, it can be helpful to provide the students with papers or cards containing words or pictures suitable for the game, so they don't have to choose their own.

GAME 14

Level: Medium / Difficult

Good for: Vocabulary review

The activity is a simplified version of the popular game Taboo.

Preparation:

Make a series of cards, each containing one word written in large letters, with a circle around it. Below that word are also written between two and four related words, written in smaller letters - these are the forbidden words.

Put one chair at the front of the room, facing towards the board. Place one to three other chairs opposite it, facing away from the board - depending on how many students are in each team.

Split the class into teams of two to four and make a table on the board to keep track of points.

Activity:

The first team comes up and sits in the chairs at the front of the class - one student is designated the role of explainer, and they sit in the chair facing the board. Their teammates are guessers, and they face away from the board. The aim of the game is for the explainer to help their teammates work what the word inside the circle is, by describing it without saying any of the forbidden words.

Once the first team has successfully guessed the word or given up, a new team comes to the front and new words are written on the board. When every team has had a go, the first team can come up again - but with a different student taking the role of explainer.

Rules:

If any of the forbidden words are used, the team gets zero points! The team with the most points wins. You can also put a time limit on describing and guessing the word (one minute is usually enough) to make things more exciting.

GAME 15

Level: Medium / Difficult

Good for: Big classes / Icebreakers / older students

Preparation:

Divide the class into groups of two to four students and give everyone a piece of paper with five questions on it - each person in a group should have different questions.

Questions should be focused around experiences, and start 'Have you ever' - for example, have you ever met someone famous? / been on the news? / danced in public? / won a medal?

Activity:

One student (A) in each group goes first, and answers one of the questions from their teammates' lists. No matter whether they have done the activity or not, they have to answer, 'Yes I have'. The other people in the group then have to ask five more questions (in any format this time) to determine whether or not student A is telling the truth - for example 'when did you do it?', 'who were you with?', or 'did you get into trouble?'

Student A's goal is to convince their teammates that they really have done what's on the card. If they haven't done it, they'll need to make up answers to the follow-up questions and trying to be as convincing as possible.

After five follow-up questions, student A secretly writes down whether the question was true or false, while their teammates write down their guess. The game then moves on, with a new teammate taking the role of student A and answering a new question.

Rules:

After everyone has answered three or more questions (depending on how much time is available), the students reveal their answers to each other. The most convincing liar wins!

289

GAME 16

Level: Medium / Difficult

Good for: Creative thinking

Preparation:

Come up with a list of problems and goals. They can be real or imaginative - from 'I am always late for class' and 'I keep losing my keys' through to 'I want to have a pet lion' or 'I wish I was rich'.

Activity:

Pick a question and write it on the board or read it out loud. Then go around the class, inviting students to give you advice on how you can solve your problem or reach your goal. Encourage creative and silly answers.

After going through a few questions, choose a student to stand up and come up with a problem or a goal of their own, again inviting the other students to suggest solutions.

If the class are struggling to get started, try going through some examples together. It's also worth reviewing correct sentence structure for answers - practicing 'I think', 'you should', 'you could try' and so on.

GAME 17

Level: Difficult

Good for: Writing practice / Group activity / Full lesson

Preparation:

Write the premise on the board and explain it to the class -

'You are now the Head Teacher of this school! You have two years to make the school perfect. You can spend as much money as you want, but everything has to be finished in two years. What will you do?'

Discuss the kinds of things students might want to think about - What changes would they make straight away, and which ones would take longer? What would they do to make it better for students, and what would they do for teachers? What would make them happier, healthier, better at studying? If students are struggling, you can put some prompts on the board, such as buildings, sports, free time, library, teachers, food, music, curriculum, schedule, etc.

Encourage them to be as specific as possible - so rather than just saying 'We should have better lunches', they should talk about what food would be on their perfect menu. It's also important to remind the students that they are the

292

headteacher in this scenario! So, cancelling all the classes wouldn't work out very well.

Activity:

Give the class 15 minutes to work individually on their answers, writing down their thoughts (they only need to write notes for their own use in this activity - so let them know their writing won't be marked). Then put them into groups of three to five and give them the rest of the lesson to share ideas within their groups and put together presentations that they will give to the class next lesson, explaining what their perfect school would look like. It can be helpful for each group to have a leader, to lead the presentation and help the group to organize their ideas.

Next lesson give the groups ten minutes to practice. They then take it in turns to deliver their presentations - with time for questions and answers at the end of each one. At the end of the final presentation, students vote on which idea of the perfect school they like best.

This activity can also be adapted to different topics - for example, the perfect town, city or country.

GAME 18

Level: Difficult

Good for: Creative writing

Preparation:

Bring a pack of cards, and a list of 13 adjectives that could describe the action in a story - one for each type of card. For example:

A - Fun

2 - Frightening

3 - Sad

4 - Romantic

5 - Crazy

6 - Exciting

7 – Heart-breaking

8 - Dramatic

9 - Unexpected

10 - Fantastic

J - Weird

294

Q - Tense

K - Dangerous

You will also need a theme for the story - something like 'Your teacher goes on vacation' or 'A girl learns magic' - choose a topic that the class will engage with, and/or which relates to recent areas of study.

Activity:

Start off by telling the beginning of the story - then hand it over to the class. Choose a student to draw one card from the pack. The number on the card will decide what type of thing will happen next. For example, it they take a 4, something romantic must happen - such as two characters falling in love, a new love interest entering the story, or someone going to a wedding.

Let students contribute their ideas by raising their hands and continue the story together. If two good suggestions are made, let the class vote on their favorite. Keep telling the story until all of the cards have been drawn - you can reduce the deck to just two suits if you have limited time.

The story must end by the end of the deck, so encourage students to wrap things up when you get down to the final cards. At the end, discuss your favorite moments together.

For more advanced students focusing on creative writing, this activity can also be done by getting students to write down their stories individually, and then sharing them at the end or in the next lesson.

GAME 19

Level: Difficult

Good for: Discussion / Creative writing

Preparation:

Ask students to think of an answer to the question 'if you could be any animal for a day, what would it be?'. Encourage them to explore fewer common options by providing them with a list of possible creatures, or by having a brief discussion first.

Activity:

Ask students to think about what a day as their chosen animal would be like. What would they do, and where would they be? How did they get there? What would they be excited about? What would they be afraid of?

Give them five minutes to write down a few sentences, using the voice of their animal - for example 'I am an arctic fox living on a glacier. It's cold, and I'm afraid that I won't find enough food to eat. I have four cubs at home, and they are hungry'.

Get the students to share their stories, then ask them to think about why they chose their animal.

Next, tell them to think about what a day in the life of their animal would be like if the animal was in captivity, and write new sentences with that in mind. You can explore other ideas here as well - for example, if they couldn't live in their home any more, or if their species was endangered.

If focusing on creative writing, encourage them to look at the differences between their first ideas and their new ones - discuss how putting a character into a new situation can change who they are and what motivates them.

Alternatively, for a discussion-focused lesson, use the topic as a launchpad for discussing subjects from global warming and hunting to the things that they appreciate in their own lives.

FREE BUSINESS ENGLISH TEMPLATES AND TONS OF FREE RESOURCES & GOODIES!

https://www.idmbusinessenglish.com/free-templates

One Last Thing...

If you enjoyed this book or found it useful I'd be very grateful if you'd post a short review on Amazon. Your support really does make a difference and I read all the reviews personally, so I can get your feedback and make this book even better.

If you'd like to leave a review then all you need to do is click the review link on this book's page on Amazon.

Thanks for reading and thanks again for your support!

Made in United States
Orlando, FL
07 November 2024

53595656R00181